The Little Black Dress

How to make the perfect one for you

Simon Henry

GUILD OF MASTER
CRAFTSMAN PUBLICATIONS

For Clive

When some said it would
be impossible – in one
small book – to take the
inexperienced sewer from
pattern making to sewing a
dress, you believed in me.

And for Martina, my muse.
When designing a perfect
little black dress, I thought
of you.

First published 2008 by
THE GUILD OF MASTER CRAFTSMAN PUBLICATIONS LTD
166 High Street, Lewes, East Sussex, BN7 1XU

Text © Simon Henry 2008
© Copyright in the Work, Guild of Master Craftsman Publications Ltd, 2008

ISBN 978-1-86108-623-5

A catalogue record of this book is available from the British Library.

Associate Publisher **JONATHAN BAILEY**
Production Manager **JIM BULLEY**
Managing Editor **GERRIE PURCELL**
Editors **LOUISE COMPAGNONE & RACHEL NETHERWOOD**
Managing Art Editor **GILDA PACITTI**
Photographer **CHRIS GLOAG**

Colour origination **GMC REPROGRAPHICS**
Printed and bound in Thailand by **KYODO NATION PRINTING**

Foreword

My whole fashion career seems to be highlighted by the little black dress. Whether it was the graduating collections from my undergraduate or masters degrees in the late 1980s – both were of little black dresses – or being asked to design a LBD collection for the internet in 2000.

Selling LBDs from my Pearce II Fionda range on a daily basis is testament to the longevity of the LBD. It's ageless, can always be reinvented and, through one's life, there will always be an occasion to revisit this fashion icon.

In 2007, whilst curating the little black dress exhibition for Brighton's Museum and Art Gallery, I was utterly amazed by everybody's unique interpretation of the LBD. To some it's long and dramatic; to others it's short, sexy and sassy; and occasionally it's just cute and very simple. For everyone, though, it's a fashion staple – a wardrobe must-have and a lifetime investment that will never let the wearer down.

Andrew Fionda

Pearce II Fionda

Contents

1

Getting Started

2

Making the Blocks

3

The Dresses

Greta p.118

Audrey p.106

Marilyn p.140

Jacket p.154

Hat p.164

Little Black Dress...

...just those three short words conjure up elegance, sophistication and style. Ask any elegant woman, 'What is the one essential piece in your wardrobe?' – most will answer, 'Ah, that's easy darling, it's my little black dress!'

When worn with a tailored jacket, the LBD will accompany a lady to the office or a business meeting; teamed with a cashmere cardigan or 'pash', it can move her to lunch with the girls. Finished with afternoon gloves and an extravagant hat, it transforms her for a wedding or even the races. And worn just by itself with elegant lingerie, it will take her to meet her lover – anywhere. In short, every woman should have their very own little black dress.

Left
THE EVER-FASHIONABLE DUKE AND DUCHESS OF WINDSOR SET SAIL FOR THE STATES IN 1954.

Right
RACQUEL WELCH ARRIVES IN STYLE FOR A FILM PREMIERE IN LONDON, IN 1966.

'If you put a black dress on, you're never inappropriate and you're never out of style.'

NICOLE MILLER

The Icon

Since these great beginnings, nearly every top designer has featured a little black dress in a collection at some point in their careers. Alexander McQueen, for whom the LBD is a regular motif, describes it as 'the embodiment of a woman's power, stark, direct and to the point'.

The power of the LBD was epitomized by Princess Diana when she wore a little black dress, designed by Christina Stambolian, to a function at the Serpentine Gallery in London on the night when Prince Charles confessed to adultery on national TV. The next morning, it wasn't Charles on the front page of world newspapers, but Diana in her LBD – dubbed the 'revenge dress'.

The dress later sold for a staggering $74,000 in 2007 at a charity auction in Florida. That is the power of a small piece of black fabric (and perhaps just a little bit to do with the lady who wore it)!

'*Scheherezade* is easy, a little black dress is hard.'

COCO CHANEL

Left
THROUGHOUT A CAREER SPANNING NEARLY THIRTY YEARS, FRENCH CHANTEUSE, EDITH PIAF WAS ASSOCIATED WITH HER SIMPLE LITTLE BLACK DRESS.

Right
RITA HAYWORTH STARRING IN THE FILM GILDA IN 1946.

A Little Black Timeline

For well over a century, designers, stylists and the women who wore their clothes have understood the power of the little black dress. This truly iconic fashion staple is as valid today as it ever was.

In the Victorian and Edwardian eras, black dresses were worn as symbol of mourning – for at least two years after a significant death. Following the death of her beloved Albert in1861, Queen Victoria famously wore black for the rest of her reign.

1861

1878

In 1878 London socialite Lillie Langtry *(above)* ignored social etiquette by wearing a black dress, soon after the death of her brother, to the seventh Viscount Ranalegh's fashionable reception. It might seem odd to us now, but this was considered to be the very height of irreverence. Spotted there by artists John Everett Millais and George Francis Miles, both went on to paint her in the infamous black outfit. Miles later published these drawings as 'penny postcards', and it soon became fashionable – if somewhat shocking – to wear black dresses.

'Fashion fades, only style remains the same.'

COCO CHANEL

The fabulous Gabrielle 'Coco' Chanel (*below*) designed a version of the little black dress. American *Vogue* instantly heralded it as the 'Ford' of dresses because – like Henry Ford's 'Model-T' car – it became an instant craze, was widely available and came in only one colour: black.

1926

1930–1945

Hollywood screen sirens of the 1930s and 1940s, dressed mostly in black gowns to make an impact on the big screen – this soon influences wider fashion.

1947

1950s

In 1947 Christian Dior launched the 'New Look' collection – a more feminine silhouette using lots of fabric. The 1950s fashion stereotype of 'poodle skirts and pony tails' imitated Dior's style.

The 1950s saw the end of war-time rationing. Designers were able to use as much fabric as they wished, and they did. Skirt shapes got fuller and the dirndl-line – utilizing many underskirts to show off the yards and yards of fabrics – was the height of fashion. But girls 'in the know' still favoured the 'pencil' skirt for its figure-hugging, shape-enhancing qualities.

The next LBD craze came in 1961 with the release of Blake Edwards' adaptation of Truman Capote's book *Breakfast at Tiffany's*, starring Audrey Hepburn (*below*) as Holly Golightly. Every elegant woman coveted the little black dress designed for Hepburn by Hubert de Givenchy. Capote originally wanted to cast Marilyn Monroe in the lead, but Hepburn's style and grace showed off Givenchy's creations to spectacular effect.

1961

1960s

The Mod generation adapted the LBD once again – the hemline became outrageously shorter with the introduction of the mini dress.

1970s

Designers such as Ossie Clark and Bill Blass saw the LBD return to looser, longer styles – popularly known as the maxi dress.

AUDREY HEPBURN

PLAYS HOLLY GOLIGHTLY, THE CRAZIEST HEROINE WHO EVER CREPT BETWEEN THE PAGES OF A BEST-SELLING NOVEL!

BREAKFAST AT TIFFANY'S

a JUROW-SHEPHERD PRODUCTION

GEORGE PEPPARD · PATRICIA NEAL · BUDDY EBSEN · MARTIN BALSAM and MICKEY ROONEY

BLAKE EDWARDS · MARTIN JUROW and RICHARD SHEPHERD · GEORGE AXELROD

TECHNICOLOR® A PARAMOUNT RELEASE

In the 1980s, the little black dress had added frills, big shoulder pads, balloon sleeves, taffetta and ties – inspired by television shows like *Dynasty* and *Dallas*. Key looks such as power dressing, the new romantic, valley girl and dancewear meant the LBD came in a variety of shapes and forms – as long as it was black!

Diana, Princess of Wales wore a Christina Stambolian LBD to a function at the Serpentine Gallery while Prince Charles publicly confessed to adultery.

Just a year after Diana's LBD the power of the black fabric shows itself again. Elizabeth Hurley – then a relatively unknown model and actress – turned up to the premier of *Four Weddings and a Funeral* with Hugh Grant, wearing a black Versace dress held together with medusa-headed gold pins. Dubbed 'that dress' by the media, she appeared on the front page of almost every newspaper the following day. The dress launched her firmly onto the 'A-list' and thus began a multi-million-dollar career.

At the 80th Oscars Nicole Kidman proved that all you need to look sensational is an LBD and bold accessory (it also helps to be dressed by Balenciaga).

| 2006 | 2008 | NOW |

In December 2006, Audrey Hepburn's notorious LBD worn in *Breakfast at Tiffany's* sold at a Christie's auction in London for a staggering £467,200. The dress (*above*) was one of three identical garments made for Hepburn; the others are kept in Paris at the Givenchy archives and Madrid at the Museum of Costume.

Simon Henry teaches <u>you</u> to design, fit and make your very own perfect little black dress!

How to Use this Book

This book is structured very simply. Start at the beginning and work your way through. Read the whole thing first so that you'll know what's coming next, that way there won't be any nasty surprises.

Instead of purchased patterns we're going to use very old couture methods to create a dress that fits you perfectly, made from our own pattern or 'body block'. Every time you read the word 'block', imagine it as your 'personal pattern'.

If you look upon this book as a course, each section or exercise is a precursor to the next. Follow the sections systematically, sewing each exercise as you go, not moving on to the next until you're confident with the current section. Read the instructions very carefully, even if you can sew don't assume that I'll be using the techniques you're accustomed to.

My method is one that I have designed and used over many years. It has been tested on a number of students, some with lots of experience and others with very little. It has been refined down so that it can be used by almost anyone. Only the other day, I asked my partner to insert an invisible zip as a way of testing out the teaching techniques. Although he hadn't used a sewing machine before, claiming that he couldn't even sew on a button, he did it perfectly on the third attempt! Now he wants to finish the entire sewing course. I've created a monster!

Don't try out these exercises alone; you will need help making your body block as well as with the fittings. I suggest that you approach the projects as a team effort. Get yourself a sewing partner.

You don't have to be an experienced machinist to use this book, although it will obviously take you longer if you haven't sewn before. But if you or a sewing partner can even sew a straight line, you'll manage.

I like the idea of groups of you getting together for fitting evenings or 'gin and pin' parties. Make an event out of it, arrange to meet regularly to help each other with fittings and so on. Perhaps one of you will find the whole process easier than others and can help the group through difficulties. Try it, mix a pitcher of martini and see how you get on.

Getting Started

'You can wear black at any time. You can wear it at any age. You may wear it on almost any occasion; a 'little black frock' is essential to a woman's wardrobe.'

CHRISTIAN DIOR

Equipment and Materials

Gather all of your equipment together before you start so you can get on with the job without stopping to look for missing items. Clear a space for yourself, lock out the children and the cat, and let's make a start.

Auction websites are also good for second-hand machines. But, if you go down this road, be sure to have it professionally serviced so that it runs smoothly and the tension is set. Buy new needles to suit individual fabrics.

Whatever you do, don't be tempted to buy an industrial machine just yet. They run too fast and you don't have the same control as a domestic one. If your machine has an adjustable speed, start with it on slow or medium until you are confident that you can control a straight stitching line – then you can gradually begin to increase speed.

Sewing Machine

As long as your machine sews both straight stitch and zigzag, you will be able to follow the methods in this book.

Over the years, I have upgraded to the most advanced machines, spending thousands of pounds on the latest computer embroidery technology. To be honest, though, most of the time I only use the straight and zigzag stitches. If you don't have a machine yet, get hold of a basic one. Your local supplier will recommend something suitable – either new or used.

Take long strips of your waste fabric and practice sewing seams with a $\frac{5}{8}$ inch (1.5cm) seam allowance. Press the seam open and check that there is no pulling or puckering. If there is, adjust the tension setting on your machine to compensate. Refer to the operating manual for individual machines as they will all vary slightly.

Overlocker or Serger

An overlocker is very useful for finishing off seams and neatening hems, but is by no means an essential piece of equipment. You can finish seams very well by using the zig ag setting on your normal machine. If you are lucky enough to have access to an overlocker, practise stitching long strips of waste fabric before pressing with a steam iron. Check that the seam is not gathered or stretched. If so, adjust the tension according to the manufacturer's instructions.

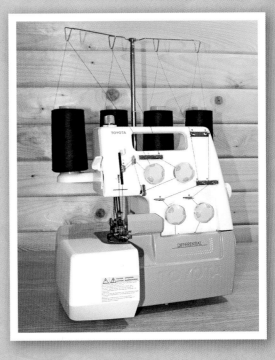

The dress stand

A dress stand or tailor's dummy isn't really necessary for this project but is helpful for doing your own fittings. A professional stand can cost up to £500 ($1000USD) and isn't even adjustable. You should be able to pick up a home-use, adjustable one for a very reasonable price – there are plenty available on internet auction sites – then you'll have it for future projects.

I use a professional one (affectionately known as Dolly), which will be used for demonstrating exercises throughout this book. As I can draw and pin directly onto 'her', it will be easier for you to understand the principles – and I don't think a live model would take very kindly to such treatment. You will also be able to better imagine the dresses on yourself if we don't use a live model.

Dress Stand

are also very helpful. They are very inexpensive and prevent sticking with even the most delicate fabrics.

You also need a sturdy ironing board with a very clean cover. I buy a new cover for each dress I make, but this is probably a bit extreme. At the very least, buy a white or natural cover as coloured ones can bleed onto your fabrics. A sleeve board, a small ironing board for pressing sleeves which fits onto your table or board, is also very useful for pressing darts open as well as getting into tight corners.

Always do a test strip for each new fabric to get the settings on your iron just right. You want the iron and steam to be just hot enough to press the seams flat, but not so hot that the fabric shrinks.

Your Iron

The importance of having a good iron cannot be stressed enough. Many a good gown has been ruined when my iron discharges its scaly contents all over lovely, pristine silk.

Whereas professional steam-generated irons were very expensive in the past, they are becoming increasingly affordable. I recently saw one on a home shopping channel for less than £70 ($140USD). A steam generator iron makes the steam in a separate tank so it is very 'dry', cutting down the chance of wetting your fabrics. Iron shields, made from heat resistant plastic that fits onto the sole plate of your iron,

Scissors

Every budding seamstress needs a good pair of scissors or tailoring shears. Make sure they are sharp and you only use them on fabric. Buy the best ones you can afford so they last for years. Mine were purchased over 15 years ago and they are still going strong!

Scissors

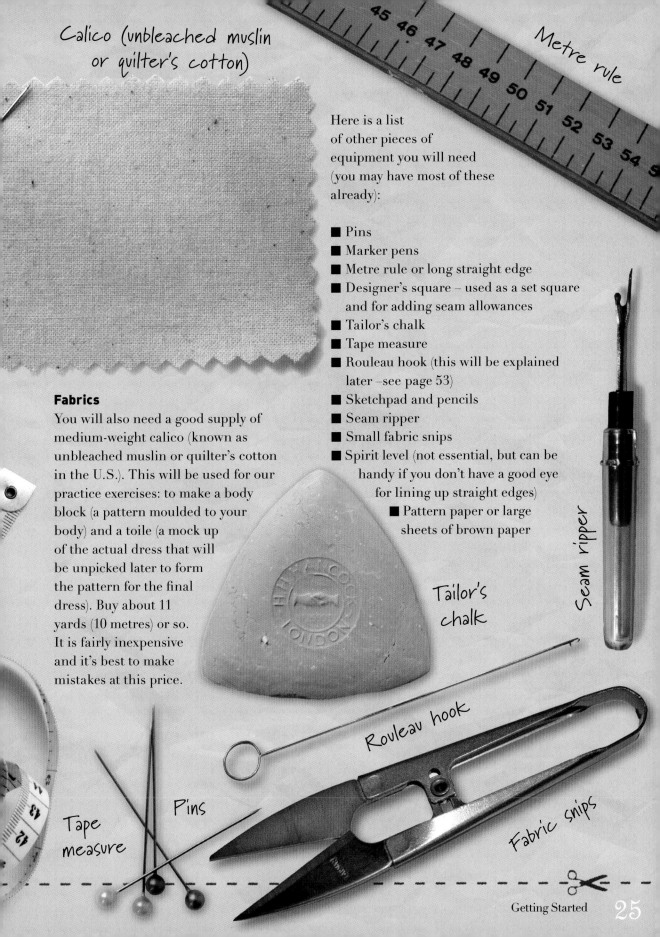

Calico (unbleached muslin or quilter's cotton)

Metre rule

Here is a list of other pieces of equipment you will need (you may have most of these already):

- Pins
- Marker pens
- Metre rule or long straight edge
- Designer's square – used as a set square and for adding seam allowances
- Tailor's chalk
- Tape measure
- Rouleau hook (this will be explained later –see page 53)
- Sketchpad and pencils
- Seam ripper
- Small fabric snips
- Spirit level (not essential, but can be handy if you don't have a good eye for lining up straight edges)
  - Pattern paper or large sheets of brown paper

Fabrics

You will also need a good supply of medium-weight calico (known as unbleached muslin or quilter's cotton in the U.S.). This will be used for our practice exercises: to make a body block (a pattern moulded to your body) and a toile (a mock up of the actual dress that will be unpicked later to form the pattern for the final dress). Buy about 11 yards (10 metres) or so. It is fairly inexpensive and it's best to make mistakes at this price.

Tailor's chalk

Seam ripper

Rouleau hook

Tape measure

Pins

Fabric snips

Sewing Techniques

This section features simple sewing techniques that are not only essential for making your little black dress, but are fundamental to nearly all sewing projects you encounter. Get them right now, and everything else later will seem easy.

Sewing a Straight Seam

This is not as straightforward as it sounds. There are several things to consider before you even touch your sewing machine.

Consider the type of fabric you are using. Thicker fabrics like calico need a different tension setting and needle size to very fine silk. Refer to the instructions that came with your machine, they will explain the different tension, pressure and needles used for different fabric weights. Every manufacturer and machine uses slightly different settings.

Make sure you use the right thread type for individual fabrics. A general, multi-purpose thread will be fine for your practice pieces, body block and toile; but you need specific thread types for different weights of fabric.

Do a test run on long strips of waste fabric or calico. This is not only good practice, but tests whether your machine tension is set up correctly.

Let's start to sew!

1 The recommended seam allowance throughout this book is ⅝ inch (1.5cm). Seam allowance is the distance that we sew in from the side edge of the garment pieces. There will be markings on the plate of your machine but, to make it easier to begin with, stick a piece of coloured tape to the base plate ⅝ inch (1.5cm) from the needle. We will call this the marker.

2 Position your fabric strips, with the 'right sides' together and the edges lined up. The 'right side' of fabric is the side that faces out on your finished garment. With patterned fabrics, for example, this will be the clear, brightly coloured side.

3 Pin the strips together at right angles to the stitching line about every 2 inches (5cm) or so. You can sew quite happily along the stitching line without removing the pins. This speeds up stitching as it eliminates the need for tacking.

4 Place the pinned strips under the needle, lining the edge up with the marker.

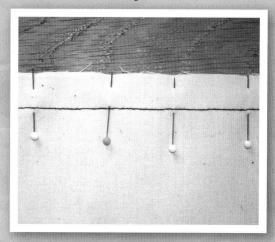

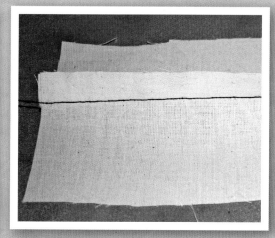

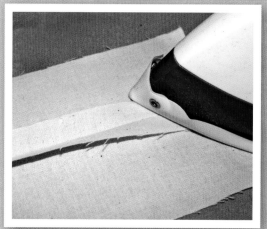

7a

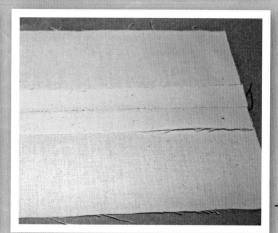

7b

5 Start stitching slowly, going forwards by two or three stitches, then push the reverse button and sew the same backwards. This will make a 'lock stitch' so that the seam will not come undone.

6 Now slowly stitch a straight line, keeping the edges of the fabric running along the marker so that you are stitching ⅝ inch (1.5cm) in from the edge. When you get to the end of the seam, sew back two or three stitches and forward two or three just as you did at the beginning of the seam. This will lock off the end of the seam.

7 Open up the seam allowance and press flat. Now, stand back and admire your own work (**7b**). Well done you!

Do a few more strips in the same way, it is a good idea to speed up a little each time until you are confident that you can sew an accurate, straight seam.

Sewing Around Curves

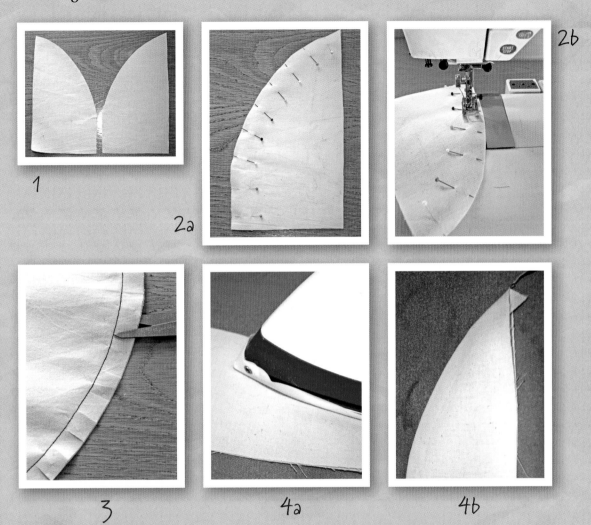

1

2a

2b

3

4a

4b

Two curves facing the same way

These can be sewn in just the same way as straight seams, keeping the edge of the fabric against the marker as you move carefully around.

1 To practise this method, cut out two identical pieces of calico: right angles joined by a curve.

2 Pin together (**2a**), and then sew (**2b**).

3 Using your sharp scissors, snip into the seam allowance to within ¹⁄₁₆ inches (2mm) of the stitching line every 2 inches (5cm) or so. This process is called 'notching', and we will be referring to it on a number of occasions during the book.

4 Turn right sides out and press (**4a**). The seam should be smooth with no sharp angles (**4b**).

2a

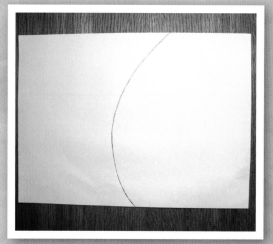

1

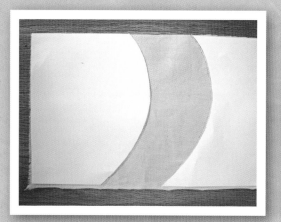

2b

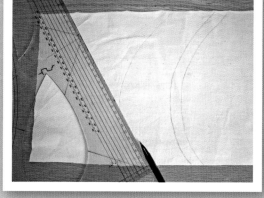

3a

One curve in and one curve out

You may want to sew a curved seam into a flat piece of fabric, such as sewing a skirt onto a curved bodice seam.

It is important to note that the stitching line should be ⅝ inch (1.5cm) in from the edge of your fabric. This is the line that you have to match when sewing the two pieces together, rather than the edge of the fabric.

Let me show you.

1 Begin by drawing a gentle curve on a piece of paper.

2 Cut along the line (**2a**) and lay it out on your piece of calico; trace around the pattern (**2b**) and mark the fabric.

3 Using your designer's set square, add a seam allowance of ⅝ inch (1.5cm) to curved edges (**3b**), then cut out the pattern pieces.

3b

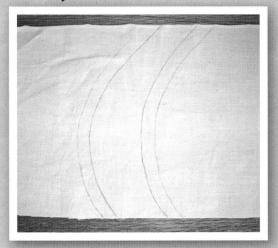

4

5a

5b

6

5 Notch (snip into it as a marker) the edge of the pieces on the stitching line, then fold in half and notch the centre line in the seam allowance on both (**5a & 5b**).

6 With the right sides together, match up the notches and pin at right angles to the seam line.

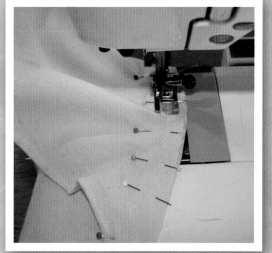

7a

7b

8

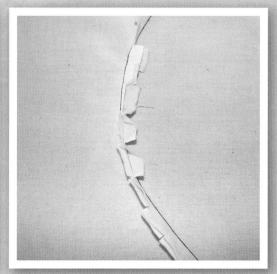

9

7 Now stitch with your machine, keeping the edge of your fabric along the marker; ease the fabric together as you go (**7a & 7b**).

8 Snip into the seam allowance, almost down to the stitching line as we did before, about 2 inches (5cm) apart.

9 Open out the curved pieces and smooth them out with your hand.

10a

10a

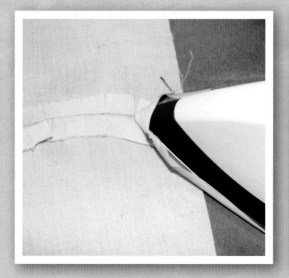

10b

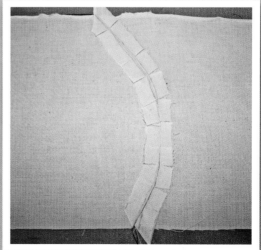

11

10 Press the seam open so that the fabric lies flat with a curved seam (**10a & 10b**).

11 Now turn over to the 'right side' of the fabric and sing yourself praise.

Repeat a few more times, using curves of different sizes, until you feel confident and understand the principle of the technique.

Once you have mastered straight and curved seams, you can pretty much sew anything. It's only a matter of practice and confidence. All of the seams described in this book will be straight, curved or a combination of both.

Darts

Darts are a way of reducing or suppressing fabric when you don't want to shape a garment using full seams. They can be either straight or curved. The classic use of darts is at the waist-to-hip suppression on skirts and trousers or the waist-to-bust, bust-to-shoulder, or hip-to-waist-to-bust-to-shoulder suppression on dresses. Some darts, like waist-to-hip or shoulder-to-bust, can be stitched in a single run. Others, like bust-to-waist-to-hip, need more than one stitching run.

We always stitch from the fullest part of the suppression before 'running off' at the smallest part. Don't worry if this sounds a bit confusing, it will become clearer in the next exercise.

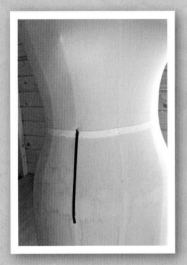
WAIST-TO-HIP

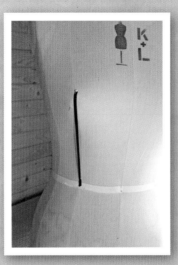
WAIST-TO-BUST

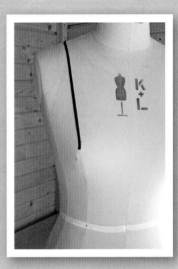
SHOULDER-TO-BUST

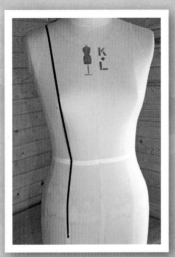
SHOULDER-TO-BUST-TO-WAIST-TO-HIP

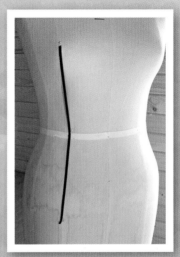
BUST-TO-WAIST-TO-HIP

1

2

3

4

A single-run dart

1 Take a square of calico and rule a line down the centre until you reach about the middle of the fabric.

2 Now measure about 1¼ inches (3cm) either side of the centre line at the top end of the fabric and make a mark.

3 Snip these marks and draw a line from the snip to the marked point on the centre.

4 Fold fabric in half along the centre line.

Getting Started   35

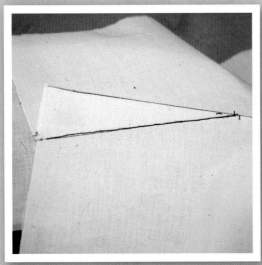

7   8

5 Matching up the snips, stitch along your marked line from the top edge to the middle.

6 Be sure to 'run off' the stitching at the end of the dart by letting the machine sew a few stitches beyond the edge of the fabric.

7 Cut the thread and tie the ends together to prevent the dart coming undone. Press to one side using either a sleeve board or the pointed end of your ironing board.

8 Flip over to reveal 'right side' of the fabric with a finished dart.

1

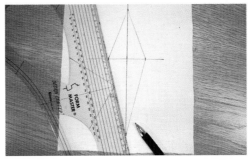
2

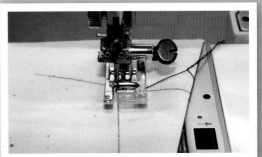
4a

3

4b

A multiple-dart run

1 Take a square of calico and rule a line down the centre as we did with the single-dart run (page 35). Place a mark half way down this line. Now, using your designer's square, draw a line at right angles to the centre line that runs about 1¼ inches (3cm) either side of the centre line.

2 Draw a dot on the centre line about 1½ inches (4cm) down from the top of the

fabric and 1½ inches (4cm) up from the bottom. Connect the dots to mark in your dart.

3 Fold the fabric in half along your centre line.

4 Stitch along the dart lines – first from the centre to the top running off at the narrowest point (**4a**), and then down from the centre to the bottom (**4b**).

5 Run off the stitching as we did before.

6 Snip into the centre of the dart (**6a**) and press to one side (**6b**).

7 Turn fabric over to 'right side' to see your finished double dart.

Oh, how clever you are!

Seam Finishes

Seams are rarely finished off in couture sewing, mostly edges are 'bagged' inside the lining. You may, however, wish to neaten and finish off the seams just in case someone gets a glimpse inside.

A

C

B

D

Overlocked edges

Overlockers are the neatest way to finish off a rough edge. They use either three or four threads that bind off the edge of the fabric, removing the rough edges as you sew (**A**).

When overlocking, be careful not to trim off too much edge fabric as this can cut into your seam allowance and alter the size of the finished garment (**B**).

Overcasting

If you don't have access to an overlocker, you can use the zigzag setting on your machine with an overcast foot – see the instruction manual for guidance (**C**).

Whilst not as neat as an overlocked edge, it's quite acceptable for the occasional straight seam (**D**).

1

2

3a

3b

French seam

On a long straight seam, such as on a long skirt, the French seam is my much favoured method of finishing. It is very neat, adds strength and body, as well as working like a 'double seam' to lock in any of the raw edges.

1 Take two long strips of waste fabric.

2 Place the 'wrong sides' together (the side of the fabric that will face the inside of your garment).

3 Stitch down the seam line using a ¼ inch (0.5cm) seam allowance (**3a & 3b**).

4a

4b

5a

5b

6

4 Press the seam open (**4a**) then fold the right sides together – the raw edges will be on the inside (**4b**) – and press again.

5 Now stitch down the pressed edge using a ⅜ inch (1cm) seam allowance, trapping the first seam inside – it sounds much more complicated than it actually is! (**5a & 5b**)

6 Now press the finished seam to one side.

Hems

A badly turned hem can ruin a beautiful dress. Think of it as wearing hoop earrings with a classic Dior evening gown. This section looks at simple but very effective methods of hem finishing.

Please note that the hem finish you were probably expecting to use the most – the turned up and then hand- or machine-stitched hem – will only be used for lining and the 'Greta' (wrap) dress in this book.

This is the by far the easiest one to get wrong. You can often see the pressing line on the 'right side', and any visible stitches or puckers will stand out like a sore thumb. Here are some pleasant alternatives.

The bagged-in hem

The bagged-in hem (**A**) is probably the simplest hem line finish. It's made by cutting out a lining the same length as a skirt, stitching around the hem and turning it through before sewing the skirt to the bodice. This method hides all the seam edges but adds bulk to the finished garment. It also works well on both full or straight skirts, in either short or long designs.

A

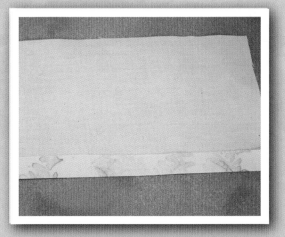

A

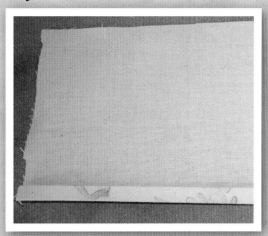

B

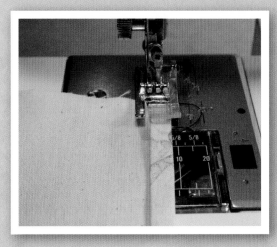

C

D

The roll-turned hem

The roll-turned hem is suitable for linings
and underskirts.

Simply press the hem ½ inch (1cm) to the
inside (**A**), then turn it down again by
¼ inch (0.5cm) making a double turn (**B**).

Sew on the wrong side, as close to the
turned edge as you can (**C**), and then press
to form a neat finish (**D**).

The bias-bagged hem

This is a really nice hem finish. It adds weight and body to a hem line and, as there is a seam line at the edge rather than a fold, is very neat. It can be used on any shaped hem and is very useful for curved hems like full circle skirts. There is some hand sewing required so it is sensible to practise many times to develop confidence.

1

2a

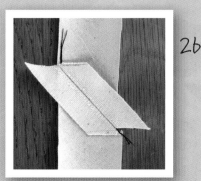

2b

3

4a

4b

To make bias strips

You can buy bias binding in cotton and satin, but it looks much nicer if you make it from the main fabric of your garment – and it's also very easy to do.

1 Lay out your fabric and rule 2 inch (4cm) lines at 45-degree angles across the fabric.

2 Cut along lines, lay the ends of two strips together at right angles and stitch. Repeat for other pieces, stitching together to make one long strip, and then press (**2a & 2b**).

3 Fold width ways by ¼ inch (1cm) and press. This will be the edge that you hand sew in place.

4 Next you need to take a practice strip of fabric about 4 inches (10cm) wide. With the 'right sides' together, stitch the unpressed edge of the bias strip to the edge of the practice piece using a ¼ inch (1cm) seam allowance (**4a-4d**).

4c

4d

5a

5b

5c

5d

5 Press the seam open then fold bias strip to the wrong side and press again (**5a**). Now hand sew in place, catching just one thread on the main fabric with each stitch (**5b-5d**).

6 Press again.

Useful Tip

The right side of a fabric is the one that will face outwards on your finished garment. With patterned fabrics, for example, this will be the clear, brightly coloured side.

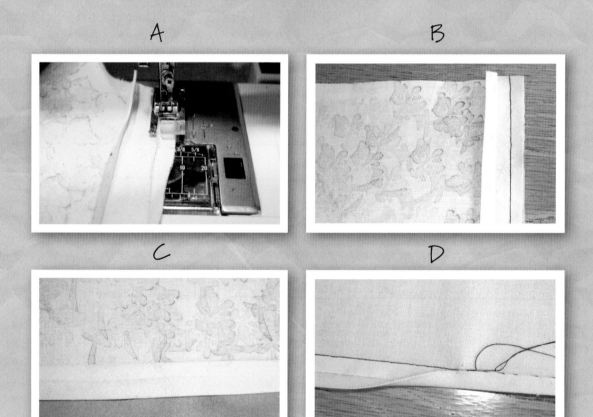

A

B

C

D

E

F

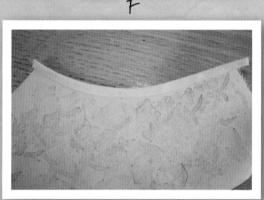

The bias-bound hem

Prepare the bias strips as described in the previous exercise. Sew the unfolded edge to the edge you want to finish using a ¼ inch (1cm) seam allowance. Now turn the folded edge of bias strip to the inside and hand stitch in place along stitching line. This will bind the edge (**A, B, C & D**).

This is a very useful technique for finishing all sorts of edges, hems, armholes, necklines and so on. As the strip is cut on the bias or cross grain, it will stretch and shrink easily and works well with curved seams (**F**).

Boned Seams

There are times when you want to add stiffness and support to seams, such as on a basque top or a corset. Adding boning to a seam is not as difficult as it may sound. Just take this section slowly, and you might just dazzle yourself with the results.

Whereas in the past boning was made out of whalebones, it is now produced from a number of materials including steel, solid polyester and (my boning of choice) rigiline, which is made from thin strands of polyester and nylon woven together. While the other types of boning slot inside a casing, rigiline is sewn directly onto the seam.

Useful Tip

As well as boning seams, you can add stiffness to any part of a garment – such as shirt collars, hooped skirts and so on.

1 Run a seam down a scrap piece of fabric and press them open.

Now set your machine to the zigzag setting and cut a length of rigiline the same length as the seam.

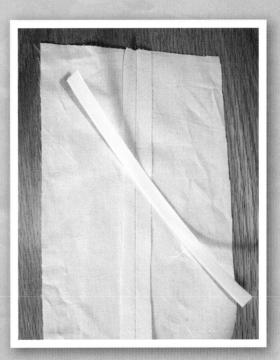

1

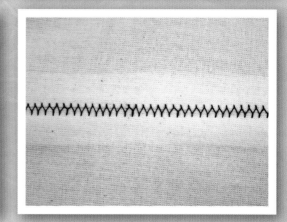

2 The ends of boning can be sharp and may poke through the main garment, so it is important to wrap the ends. Cut small squares of scrap fabric and place a square over the end of the bone.

3 Lay boning along the seam line on the 'wrong side' and zigzag down, making sure you stay over the stitching line. Finish by placing another square of scrap fabric over the end of the bone (**3a, 3b & 3c**).

Fastenings

In much the same way as hems, badly inserted fastenings can spoil otherwise elegant and beautifully finished garments. Paying attention to details pays off! This section explores a number of different fastenings – from zips to rouleau loops.

Zips

The easiest but best-looking fastening of all is the concealed zip. From the outside it looks like another seam, but concealed zips are slightly different from normal zips as the slider is on the opposite side.

1

To insert an invisible zip

As with many other sewing techniques in this book, this is process is much simpler than it seems. As soon as you have added an invisible zip, you will get the principle and never use a normal zip again.

Buy a few 8 or 10 inch (20 or 25cm) concealed zips from your local sewing shop, remembering they are different to normal zips.

1 Take two pieces of scrap fabric and place onto the table with the 'right sides' facing up. Now undo the zip. The right side (front) actually looks more like the wrong side (back) of the zip.

With the wrong side facing up, open the zip fully and place the right-hand tape onto the left piece of fabric – make sure the end of the tape is at the top of the fabric.

You will find that you can roll open the 'teeth' on the wrong side of the zip just by holding the tape flat to the fabric with your right hand, and rolling the teeth to the left. We are going to sew in this crease line.

2

3

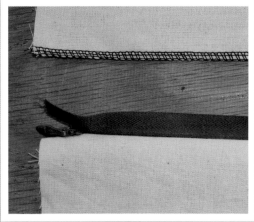

4

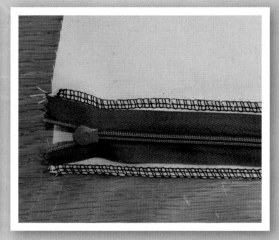

5

2 Attach the zipper foot to your machine (see manufacturer's instructions) so that the needle is on the left side of the foot.

3 With the edge of the zipper tape ¼ inch (0.5cm) in from the edge of the fabric, roll open the 'teeth' slightly. Now, stitching in the crease line, sew down to about ¾ inch (2cm) from the 'stop staple' at the bottom of the zip. Remember to do a lock stitch at the start and end.

4 Close the zip. Now tuck the seam under, folding the zipper tape to the 'wrong side' of the fabric. Place it along side the second piece of fabric and flip it over so that the fabric right sides are together.

5 Undo the zip.

6

7a

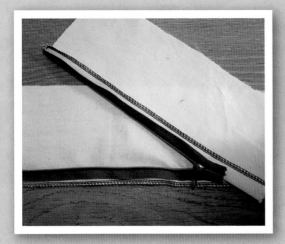

7b

8

6 Move the zipper foot so that the needle is on the right-hand side of the foot.

7 Sew down the zipper tape, just as you did for the first side (page 50), making sure you stop ¾ inch (2cm) from the 'stop staple' at the bottom of the zip (**7a & 7b**).

8 Open up the work so that the 'right side' is facing up. Now do up the zip so that it looks like a normal seam.

9

10a

10b

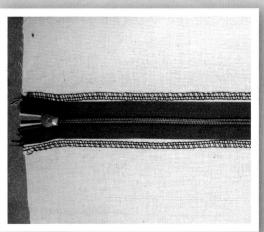

11

9 Fold all of the fabric right sides together and, leaving the zipper foot in the same position, stitch down from where the stitching line stops.

Be very careful not to catch the zipper tape by folding the zip in half and pulling it slightly out of the way as you stitch down.

10 Press the seam open on the wrong side of the fabric and press over the zip on the right side (**1a & 1b**).

11 Insert several zips using this very same technique until you're confident with the entire procedure.

Buttons and Rouleau Loops

A rouleau is a thin strip of bias-cut fabric that is seamed down one side, then turned through to make a 'tube'. These are often used as loops for buttons or lacing, as well as for straps on tops, dresses and lingerie.

Buttons and loops create a very nice effect, especially when you place the buttons close together. You can place a row of buttons and loops down the back of a dress, a few on a cuff or one as a back neck fastening.

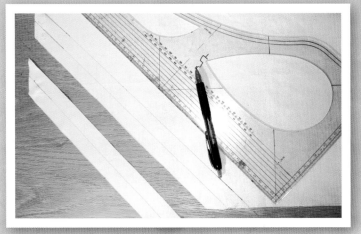

1a

1b

2a

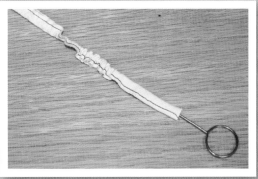

2b

How to make rouleau loops

1 Lay out your fabric and mark bias strips of ¾ inch (2cm). Cut out the strips then, working each one in turn, fold in half along width. Stitch in from the folded edge using a ⅜ inch (0.5cm) seam allowance (**1a & 1b**).

2 Using a rouleau turner (a thin length of wire with a loop at one end and a latch-hook at the other) push the hook end inside the rouleau and grab the top end of the rouleau (**2a & 2b**).

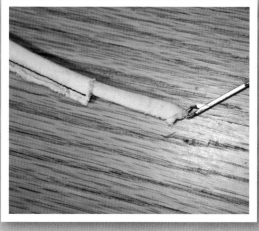

3a

3b

4a

4b

3 Very slowly and carefully pull through by turning the rouleau right side out (**3a & 3b**).

4 Take the required button size and then measure around the circumference. Add 1¼ inch (3cm) to this figure and you will have the precise measurement for cutting your rouleau loops (**4a & 4b**).

5

6

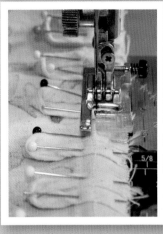

7a

7b

8

5 Cut two strips of waste fabric to a width of 4 inches (10cm). Notch markings down one side, ¾ inches (2cm) apart.

6 Fold one rouleau loop in half, line up the raw edges with the edge of your fabric (right side up) on the notched mark and pin them into place.

7 When all loops are in position, run a line of stitching ⅜ inch(1cm) in from the edge of the fabric to secure (**7a** & **7b**).

8 Remove pins. Place second strip of fabric over the first with the 'right sides' together. This is called the 'facing' – it traps all of the loops in between the two layers of fabric.

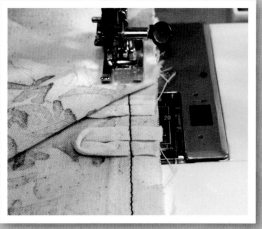

9

10a

10b

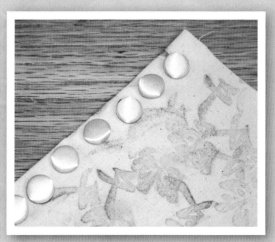

11a

9 Stitch down the fabric using a ⅝ inch (1.5cm) seam allowance.

10 Fold the 'facing' around to the back of the work, exposing the loops, before pressing (**10a & 10b**).

11 'Face' a second strip of fabric – as in the previous step, but without the rouleau loops – and press. Lay the looped and plain pieces side-by-side and sew on the buttons to correspond with the loops (**11a & 11b**).

11b

The Little Black Dress

Lacing

Lacing up the back of a corset or basque top can be a very effective technique. It allows a little ease for fitting a garment, as it can be either laced looser or tighter depending on the wearer.

Lacing works best on boned garments, but is occasionally used for fastening skirts or cuffs. You need to make either holes or eyelets in a fabric in order to thread the lacing through; there are several ways to do this. Eyelets and suitable tools to apply them directly to fabric can be purchased from haberdashery stores. I tend not to use this method as it often splits the fabric and the holes can fray.

You can also buy eyelet tape, which has strong eyelet holes already made. It's quite effective on corsets, but I would only use this method if the tape isn't going to show on the finished garment.

The third, and my preferred method of lacing, is to use rouleau loops and ribbon or lacing cord.

Apply the loops, but don't make them as long as you did in the previous exercise. Ensure that the loops are evenly spaced and that you have the same number on both sides. Lace up with cord (**A & B**).

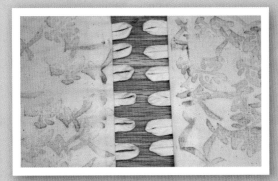

A

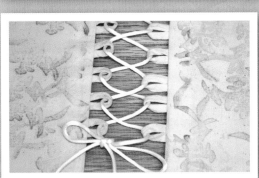

B

Now we're ready to get started. That's pretty much all of the sewing techniques you will need to sew your very own little black dress.

At this stage, it is advisable to go back and re-do the exercises that you didn't feel comfortable with. Make sure that you are confident using all of the techniques before you go any further.

Now we'll look at how to make a pattern.

Making the Blocks

'You have to wear black, aging or not, because when a little black dress is right, there is nothing else to wear in its place.'

WALLIS WARFIELD SIMPSON, DUCHESS OF WINDSOR

The Body Block

A body block is a fabric rendition of half your exact body shape. It is the starting point for a pattern and is very important in regards to fitting your dress perfectly. Get this part right and it will save you a lot of time adjusting the toile later.

You won't be able to create a body block on your own. Find a sewing partner to help.

You will need:
- A tape measure
- A designer's square
- Calico
- Marker pen with a fine tip
- Pins
- Elastic
- A spirit level – this isn't essential but is helpful if you can't line things up with your eye
- A very tight-fitting white t-shirt (buy a size too small so it fits very tightly). Fold the t-shirt in half (**A**) down the centre front and draw a line (**B**) with your felt-tip pen to mark. Do the same (**C**) down the centre back.

You will now need to take seven measurements:
- Bust
- Hips
- Nape of the neck to just blow the buttocks
- Bust point to bust point (nipple to nipple)
- Shoulder blade to shoulder blade
- Above shoulder to bust point
- Above shoulder to shoulder blade point.

Write these measurements down carefully.

Important note:
If your hip measurement is larger than your bust measurement, you will have to make a separate bodice block and skirt block. Follow the instructions for the bodice to the waist, then do the same for the skirt. When you have finished, join the bodice pieces to the corresponding skirt pieces.

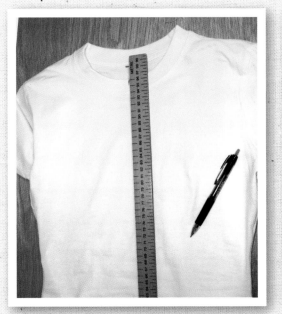

A

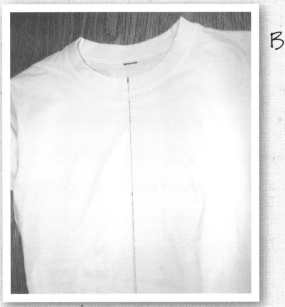

B

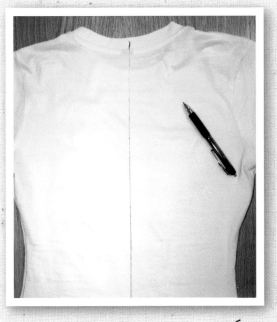

C

Useful Tip

A toile is a mock-up of the actual dress, which will be unpicked to form the pattern for the real thing.

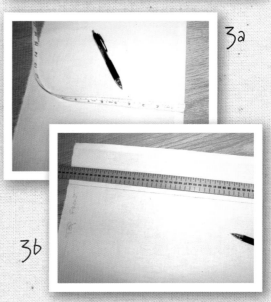

1 Cut two strips of calico. The width should be ¼ of the bust or hip measurement – the largest of the two – plus 4 inches (10cm); the length should be the nape of the neck to below the buttock measurement plus 4 inches (10cm) (**1a**). Now fold back ⅜ inch (1cm) of fabric down one of the long edges and press (**1b**).

2 Place the two strips down with the turn of the left piece on the left side and the turn of the right piece on the right. Write 'top' on the top edge of both pieces, 'front' on the right piece and 'back' on the left.

3 Working with the front piece, measure in from the folded edge (**3a**) by ½ of the nipple to nipple measurement.

Do this in a couple of places and draw a line through the points, making sure it is parallel to the folded edge of the fabric (**3b**). If are modelling the top and skirt separately, you also need to measure the same amount in from the skirt centre front.

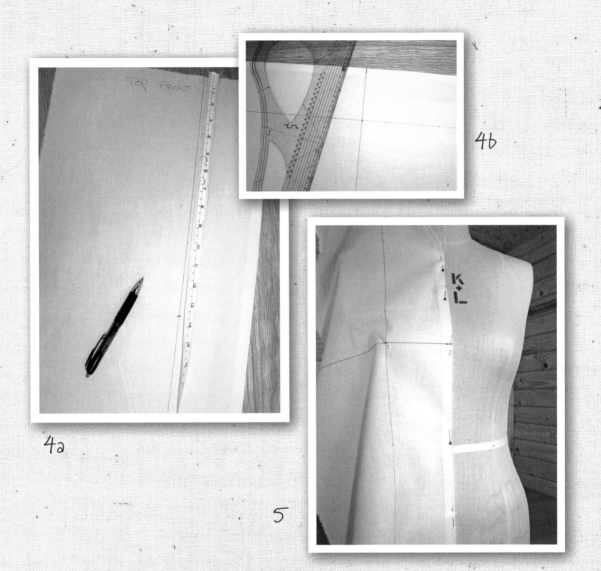

4a

4b

5

4 Now measure down from the top of this line – the above shoulder to bust point measurement – and mark (**4a**). This will be your bust point.

Using the designer's square, draw a line at right angles to the first line cutting through the bust point mark (**4b**).

5 Pin the bust point mark to the model's bust-point (be very careful) then pin the folded edge to the centre line on the t-shirt, keeping the bust line horizontal.

6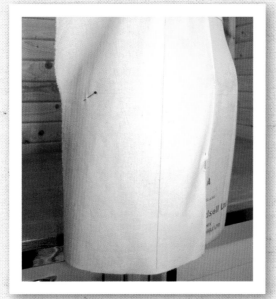

7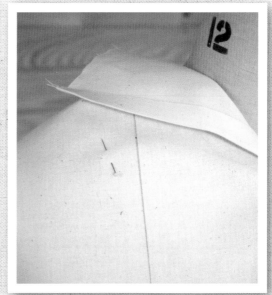

8a

8b

6 With the flat of your hand, smooth the fabric across the hip and pin at the side.

7 Smooth the fabric up from the bust and pin to just below the shoulder.

8 We are now going to mark in the neckline with your sharp scissors. Being careful not to cut your model, point the scissors upwards, place the scissor point to the left of the neckline and snip up. (**8a**).

This will free up some of the fabric, making it sit closer to the body (**8b**).

9a

9b

9c

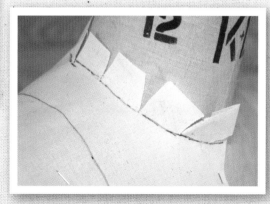

10a

9 Continue this method all around the neck to the shoulder seam (**9a, 9b & 9c**).

10 Now that the block sits close to the neck, mark around the neck shape and cut away any excess fabric. Pin to hold at the neck edge of the shoulder (**10a & 10b**).

10b

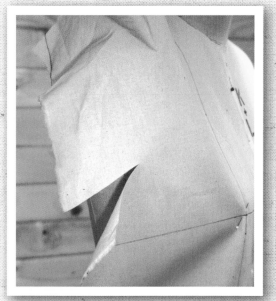

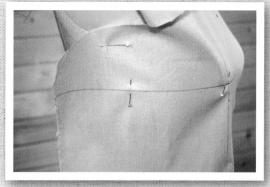

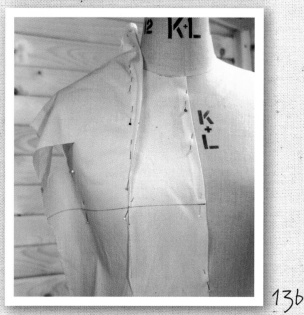

11 We are now going to insert the shoulder to bust point dart. Cut a line from the side seam, close to the arm pit, to the armhole seam on the t-shirt – this will free up some of the fabric.

12 Look at the bust line and straighten it so it runs absolutely horizontal – some find it easier to use a spirit level here – and pin the line to the side seam.

13 Take out the pin holding the block up at the shoulder. With the flat of your hand, smooth the fabric upwards from the bust. Fold fabric along the vertical line and pin the resulting dart into place as close to the body as you can without stretching the t-shirt. Pin to hold the shoulder in place. (**13a & 13b**).

Note: You can pin this dart in anywhere on the shoulder but, for now, centre it on the line drawn in earlier. For very full-busted models, just pin the dart in where the most natural fall of the fabric seems to be.

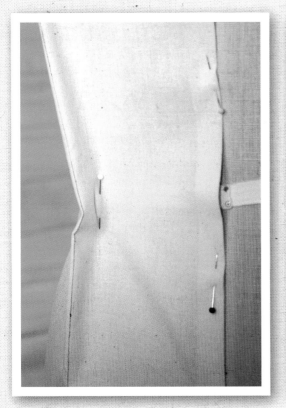

14a

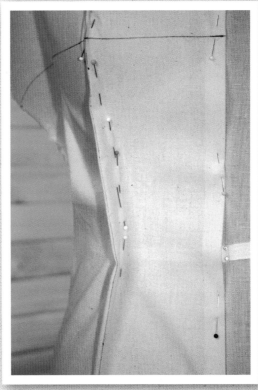

14b

15

14 We are now going to suppress the waist dart up to the bust and down to the hip. Folding on the line – as we did with the bust dart – pin out the fullness at the waist. (**14a & 14b**).

15 Carry on up to the bust point then down to the hip in the same manner, fitting close to the body but being careful not to stretch the t-shirt. If you are modelling a separate top and skirt block, you only need to model the waist and later make the skirt as a separate piece.

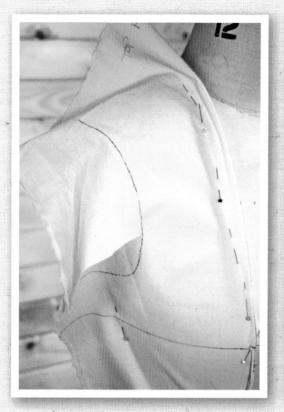

16a

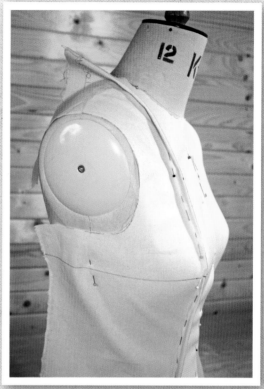

16b

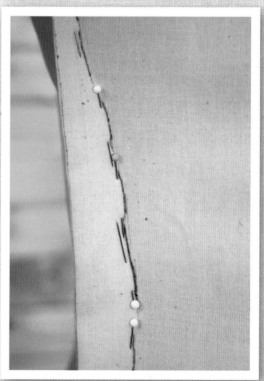

17

16 Mark around the armhole seam – from the edge of the shoulder to the under arm – and trim away any excess fabric.

17 Mark in both sides of all darts, following the pin lines.

The front block is finished for the time being. Now we will repeat the process on the back block in the same order.

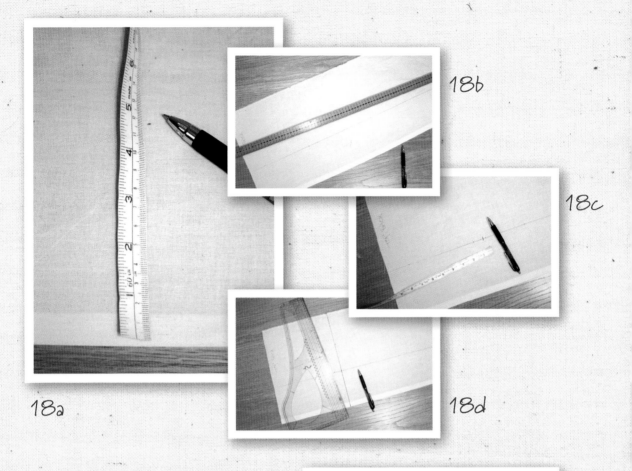

18a

18b

18c

18d

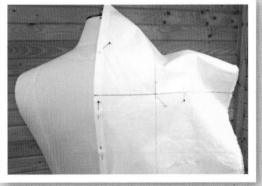

19

18 Take the back piece that we cut earlier. Measure in the blade-to-blade measurement from the folded edge of the fabric and make a mark (**18a**).

Draw a line parallel to the folded edge running through this mark (**18b**).

Measure down this line from the top – the above-shoulder-to-blade measurement – and mark; this is the blade point (**18c**).

Draw a line at right angles to the first line, cutting through the blade point (**18d**).

19 Pin the blade-point to the shoulder blade and the centre back to the centre-back line on the t-shirt. Insert a pin to hold the shoulder line up, making sure the blade line is absolutely horizontal. Smooth fabric out to the hip and pin at the side seam.

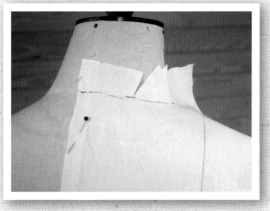

20a

20b

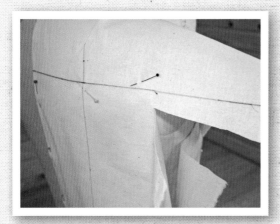

21a

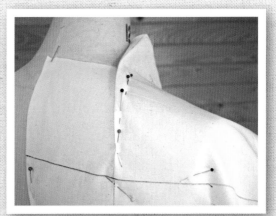

21b

20 Snip into the back neck line as we did for the front; then mark and trim (**20a**). Now pin the fabric at the neck edge of the shoulder (**20b**).

21 Cut in from the side seam – close to the arm pit – right up to the armhole seam on the t-shirt (**21a**).

Pin under the arm, keeping the blade line horizontal. Smooth the fabric upwards and pin out the shoulder dart (**21b**).

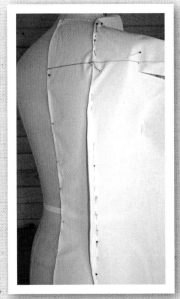

24

22 Pin out the waist dart – up to the blade point and down to the hip – just as we did for the front. Do this on separate pieces if you are modelling a separate top and skirt (**22a & 22b**).

23 Mark the armhole, making sure to follow the armhole seam on the t-shirt, and cut away any excess fabric.

24 Pin in the shoulder line, pinning the back to the front and keeping as close to the shoulder as you can. Trim away the extra fabric.

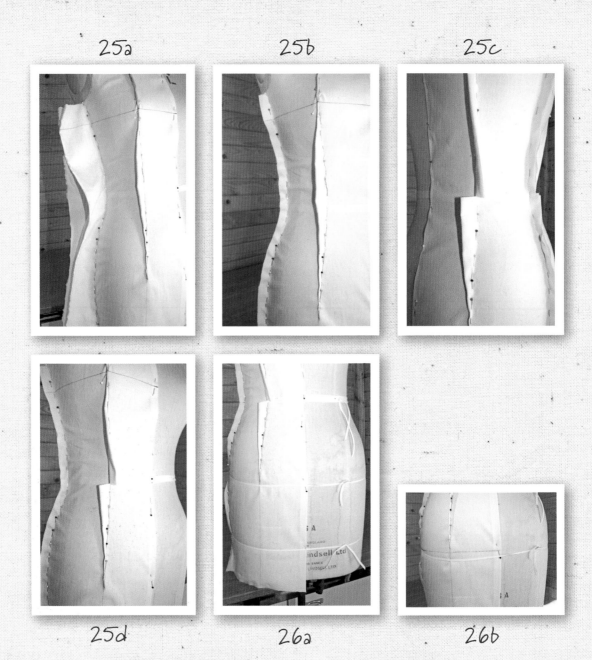

25a 25b 25c

25d 26a 26b

25 With the model's arm bent and slightly out to the side – and the elbow in line with the slope of the shoulder – remove the pins at the hips and underarm.

Pin the side seams in, keeping as close to the body as you possibly can without stretching the t-shirt (**25a**). Cut away any excess fabric (**25b**).

Mark in both sides of all darts as we did for the front. Snip into the waist darts to relax the fabric ever so slightly – this step isn't necessary if you are making a separate top and skirt block (**25c & 25d**).

26 Tie a length of elastic around the waist – one around the hips and one close to the bottom of your block (**26a & 26b**).

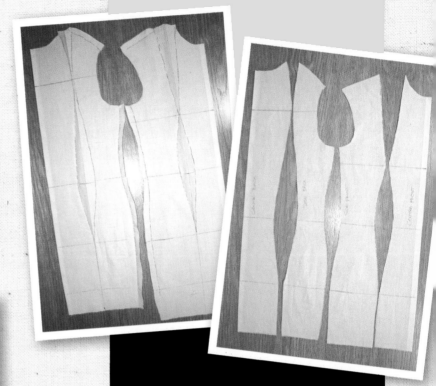

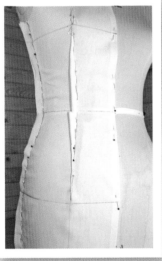

26c

Making sure that each piece of elastic is absolutely horizontal, mark lines around the body block using the elastics as guides – use your spirit level if you need to (**26c**).

You have now finished half of the block modelling. Remove the block from your model and take out the pins. If you have ever used a purchased paper pattern, this will look very familiar.

Take out all pins and cut on the dart and seam lines. You will now have four pattern pieces: centre front, side front, side back and centre back. If you are modelling the blocks separately, join the top pieces to corresponding skirt pieces using sticky tape. Mark the piece names onto the block: centre front, side front, side back and centre back.

We are now going to make and fit a full body block from these pattern pieces.

Full Block

Your body block is the key to creating a beautifully fitting little black dress. Don't carry on to the next stage of the design process until you've made one that fits you perfectly. It's worth taking the time to get this critical stage of the process right.

Before we start, I need to say a few words about fabric grain. The threads of a fabric run top to bottom and side to side. To give the garment structure and body, always cut along on the 'straight grain'. To make a garment soft and draped, cut along the 'cross grain' or bias – this runs diagonally across the grain. Cross or bias cutting can be very difficult; as the sewing techniques are too advanced for beginners, they have not been explored in this book.

Let's start to cut and sew.

Before doing anything, make sure the calico isn't creased. I always press fabric before starting a project.

1

Useful Tip

Selvedge is the edge of the fabric woven to prevent unravelling.

Fold a piece of calico – long enough to fit all your body block pieces – in half across the width. Fold the selvedge to the selvedge so that the fold will be on the 'straight grain'.

1 Lay the folded fabric out on your cutting area – a table or, if you don't have room, the floor – with the folded edge towards you. Lay the folded edge of the centre-front piece along the fold of your fabric and pin into place.

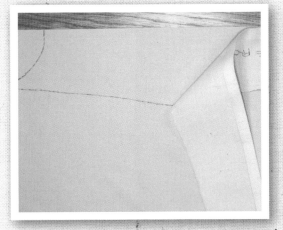

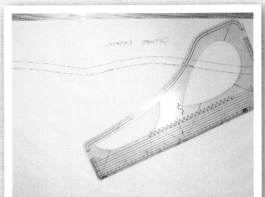

4

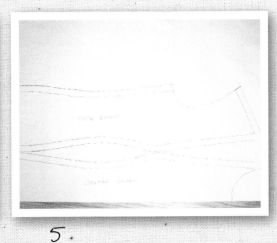

5

2 Mark around the pattern piece before removing it from the fabric.

3 We now need to add a seam allowance. Using the designer's square, mark ⅝ inch (1.5cm) outside the pattern piece on the side and the shoulder seams.

4 Draw a line at right angles to the fold line of the calico, level with the hip line on your centre-front block piece. Place the side-front pattern piece next to the centre-front piece, with the hip line running along the one you just drew in. This will make the pattern piece sit on the straight grain of the fabric.

5 Leave room for your seam allowance; mark around it and then add some seam allowance to the shoulder and side seams.

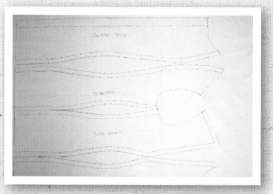

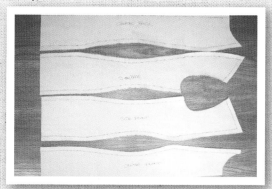

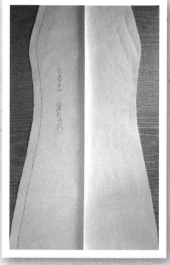

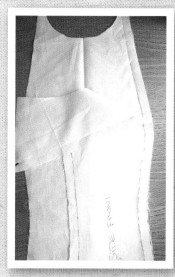

8a

8b

8c

6 Repeat for the side-back and centre-back pieces, placing the hip line on the line already drawn in – as before. Add a 1¼ inch (3cm) seam to the centre-back line to provide a little room to pin. As with your half block, add a label to each piece.

It doesn't matter if you can't manage to lay the pieces side by side, but it saves on fabric if you can. It is important to make sure that the pattern pieces are on the 'straight grain' of the fabric.

7 Cut out the block pieces on the lines. Now we are going to sew the pieces together to form the body block. Don't use a locking stitch at the beginning or end of the seams as we are going to undo them later.

8 Take the centre-front piece, open it up and place the side front, bust line seams and right sides together (**8a, 8b & 8c**). You will be stitching along the first line drawn onto the half block (page 60). Matching the stitching lines, sew a ⅝ inch (1.5cm) seam from the shoulder edge to hip edge.

9

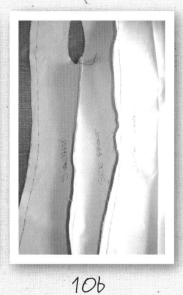

10a

10b

11a

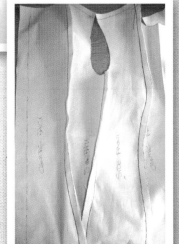

11b

9 Repeat with second side-front piece.

10 With right sides together, place the side back and side front seams together and sew, starting from under the arm down to the hip (**10a & 10b**). Repeat this process for other side-back.

11 Now take the centre-back pieces and, with right sides together, sew down from the shoulder to the hip (**11a & 11b**).

12a

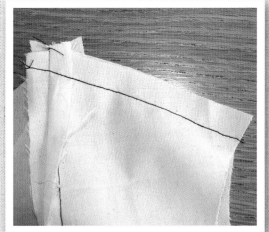

12b

Now take the right-hand shoulder seams, making sure the right sides are placed together, and sew (**12a & 12b**). Do the same for the other shoulder.

Finally, snip into the curved seams and press to complete the block (**13a & 13b**).

13a

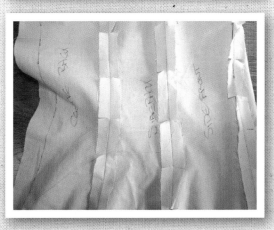

13b

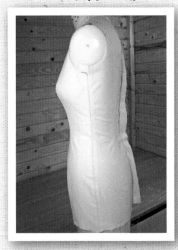

14a

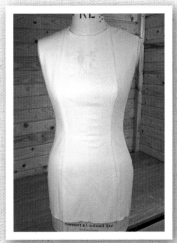

14b

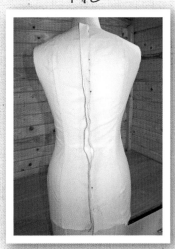

14c

Fitting the body block

Unless you're a contortionist, you'll need some help when fitting the body block. Place it onto your model, wearing only the foundation garments rather than the t-shirt. It should fit the body tightly. Pin down the back seam as close to the body as you can, being careful not to pull or stretch the block. If everything works as it should, the pinning line will be on the line you drew onto the centre back (**14a, 14b & 14c**).

Look closely at the way the block fits. Is the fabric bunching up anywhere?

If the fit isn't perfect, pin down the wrinkles and creases before marking. Unpick your block on the seams – leaving the new pins in – and re-mark, sewing a new body block from this one. Remember that the seam allowance is already marked so it shouldn't take you as long this time.

Try it on again. This time it will fit like a glove. I told you it was worth taking the time to get it right!

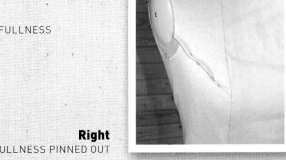

Left
TOO MUCH FULLNESS OVER BUST

Right
FULLNESS PINNED OUT

The Sleeve Block

More of my students have trouble with sleeve blocks than anything else. For some reason, they get it into their head that it's difficult and there's no persuading them otherwise. It isn't hard if you follow the instructions carefully.

If you look at a sleeve, it's only a tube with a bit of shape at one end. Go through the process step-by-step, measure accurately and you will be fine.

As we are drafting from your own body block, the sleeve measurements will be different for each individual.

There are many ways of drafting a sleeve block, but I won't confuse you with them. The technique in this section should work for everyone. It is just a simple, straight, one-piece sleeve, but is ideal for the dresses in this book if you choose to add sleeves. When drafting simple set-in sleeves for my clients, this is exactly the method I use.

A term that will come up frequently in this section is 'ease'. Ease is the amount of extra fabric added depending on how tight or loose you want the finished sleeve.

We will start off the process by using a 1½ inch (4cm) ease measurement for our basic block. You can always add or subtract at the toile stage to produce a different sleeve shape. Using the techniques described below, you will find that the more ease you add to the bicep measurement, the lower the sleeve head will be. It is unlikely that you will use this exact pattern for your dress. We are going to draft a pattern that

fits into your body block. This would be too tight to wear, but the principles are exactly the same when drafted from the toile of your actual dress.

You need to take a few measurements before we start:
- Shoulder point to wrist
- Shoulder point to elbow
- Around the bicep plus the ease measurement
- Around the elbow plus the ease measurement
- Around the wrist plus the ease measurement – make sure that this total measurement is larger than around the fullest part of your hand, otherwise you will not be able to slip the sleeve on.

Useful Tip

It is always necessary to add some ease, otherwise you won't be able to get the sleeve on. The only exception is if you want a skin-tight finish.

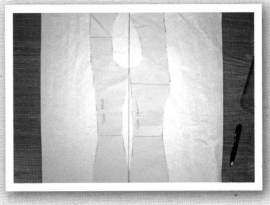

1 Lay your first body block on the table in front of you – that's the one without additional seam allowance. With your tape measure on its edge, measure around the back armhole from shoulder point to under arm on the very edge of the block (**1**). Now do the same for the front armhole. We are going to draft the first pattern on paper.

2 Lay out a piece of pattern or brown paper – longer than your arm and about the same width – on the table (or floor) in front of you. Draw a line all the way down the centre of the paper. This will become the centre line of your sleeve. The left-hand side of this line will become the back of the sleeve and the right-hand side will become the front.

3 Place the front and back body blocks together at the side seam. Position them with the join on the centre line and highest shoulder point at the top of the paper.

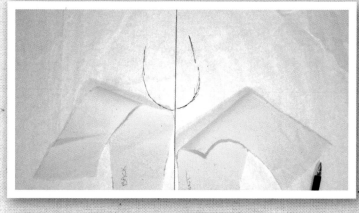

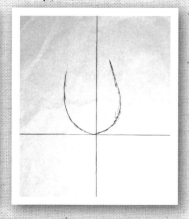

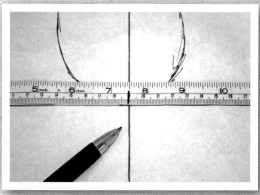
5

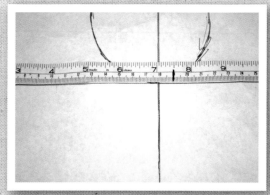
6

4 Mark around the armhole, stopping three-quarters of the way up to the shoulder edge, then draw a line at 90 degrees to the centre line at the bottom point of the armhole. We will call this the bicep line.

When you measured the front and the back armholes, you should have found that the front measures more than the back. Take the difference between the two measurements and halve it. In the case of my block, the back measurement was 8 inches (20cm) and the front measurement was 8¾ inch (22cm). There was a difference of ¾ inch (2cm), half of this is ⅜ inch (1cm). This is the amount that we need to offset the centre point by – the measurement will differ depending on your body block.

5 Take your bicep measurement and mark half way along the centre line.

6 Now move the tape measure to your right – the distance of your offset measurement – and mark the bicep measurement onto the bicep line.

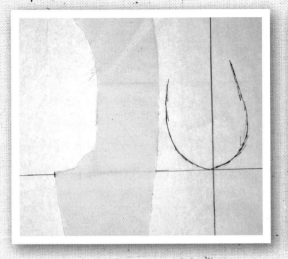

9a

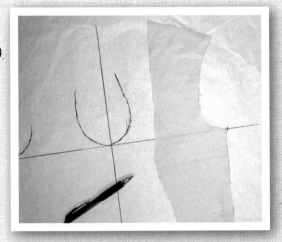

9b

7 Place the corner point of the side seam and armhole of the back body block onto the left-hand mark that you just made.

8 Now trace around a quarter of the armhole shape.

9 Repeat for the right-hand side using the front block (**9a & 9b**):

As the underarm shape is now drawn into our sleeve, let's to draw in our sleeve head.

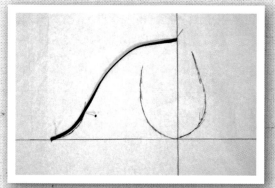

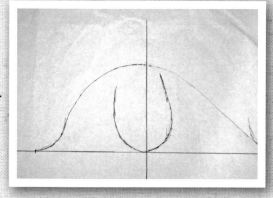

10 Take a piece of cord and cut it to the exact same length as the back armhole measurement we took earlier. Place one end of the cord on the left-hand bicep mark and, following the start of the armhole line that we just drew in, make a nice curve up to the centre line.

11 Now draw in this line. Repeat for the front sleeve, using a new piece of cord cut to the front armhole length.

12 Make sure that the curves flow and the top of the sleeve head is not too pointy. Keep drawing in the curves until they flow very smoothly.

There are formulas for doing this, but they would be too difficult for you at this stage.

Just keep trying until the curves look about right. You can always go back and draft another sleeve block if you are unhappy with the result.

It usually takes me two or three attempts to make the line run smoothly. You may find the curves on you designer's square to be useful for this.

13 Measure around the sleeve head with the edge of your tape measure. This should be the same as the back armhole plus the front armhole measurement. If not, adjust accordingly, making sure the shape still flows nicely.

Your sleeve head should now be drawn in successfully.

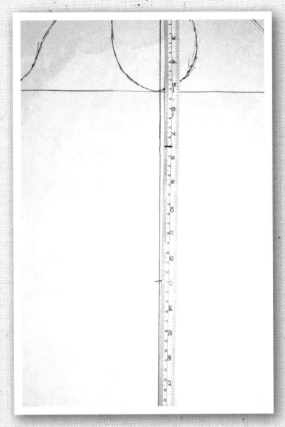

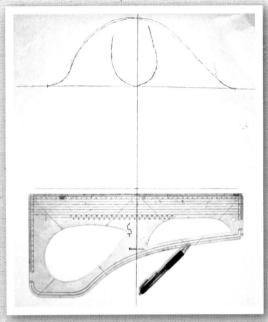

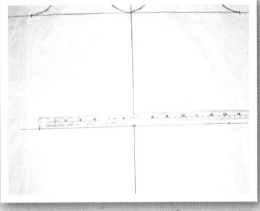

16a

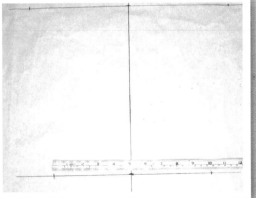

16b

14 Now we will take the shoulder to elbow measurement – down the centre line from the top of the sleeve head – and mark this in. Next, mark in the shoulder to wrist measurement – from the very top of the sleeve head.

15 Draw lines at right angles to the centre line, passing through these marks.

16 Mark in the elbow and wrist, measuring your ease respectively on these lines, using the centre line as the central point of your measurements (**16a & 16b**).

17a

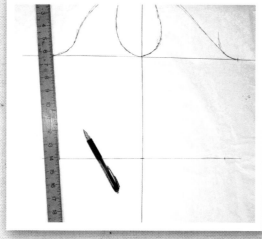

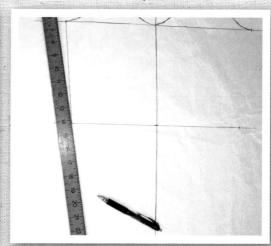

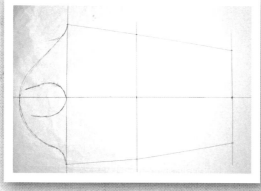

18

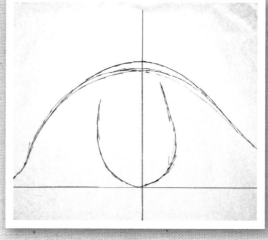

19

17 Join marks with ruled lines (**17a & 17b**). You will find that the front line curves in slightly, while the back line curves out. This is because of the offset bicep line – marked in earlier. It makes the sleeve hang slightly forwards and creates a better fit as well as a natural line on the finished sleeve.

Now, round off any sharp angles slightly to give a gentle flowing line to both sides.

18 Join up the wrist line. Measure down each side to check that both are exactly the same measurement. If not, adjust accordingly.

At the sleeve head, we need to add some ease so that there is a little fullness in this area.

19 On the centre line at the top of the sleeve, mark a point approximately ⅜ inch (1cm) up from the top of the sleeve head. Redraw the top part of the sleeve head to this point, ensuring the curve flows gently.

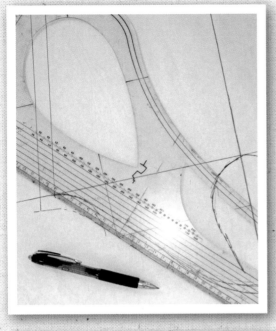

20a

20b

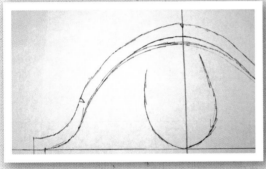

21

20 Now mark in a ⅝ inch (1.5cm) seam allowance around whole sleeve (**20a & 20b**) – be careful to follow the same curve.

21 Draw or cut little 'v' shapes at the centre line along the top – this will become the shoulder point mark. Place a 'v' anywhere on the back (left-hand) sleeve head seam so that it's possible to identify the back after cutting it out.

YOUR FINISHED
SLEEVE BLOCK

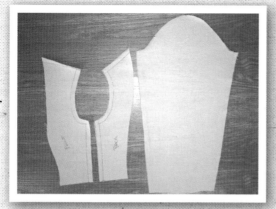

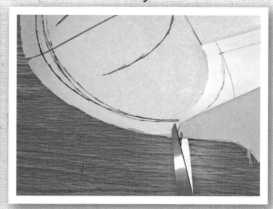

23

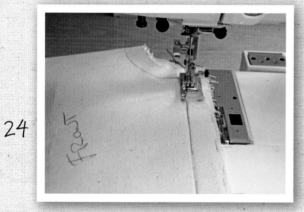

24

25a

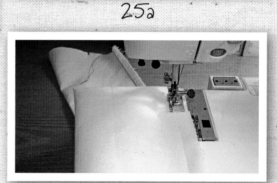

25b

25c

22 Now let's see if the sleeve fits. Using your calico, cut out one side-back block piece and one side-front piece, adding seam allowances to the side, shoulder and armhole seams.

23 Cut out one sleeve using the pattern we just made, snipping into the 'v' notches to mark this point.

24 Sew the shoulder and side seams of the body block; press open using a sleeve board and turn through to the 'right side'.

25 Fold the sleeve in half and sew down the sleeve seam. Ensure the notch marking the back of the sleeve is at the back armhole seam (**25a, 25b & 25c**).

26

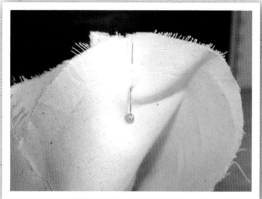

27

28

29a

26 Hold the body block with the seams on the outside, place the sleeve on the inside of the body block so that the right sides are together. Pin the side seam and sleeve seams together at the under arm.

27 Now pin the notch at the sleeve head to the shoulder seam.

28 At right angles to what will be your stitching line, pin the sleeve head into place, easing in slightly around the top of the sleeve head.

29 Next, stitch around the inside of this seam using a ⅝ inch (1.5cm) seam allowance (**29a & 29b**).

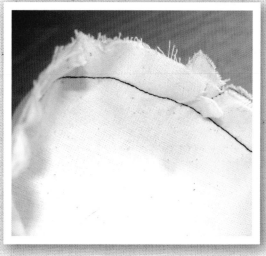

29b

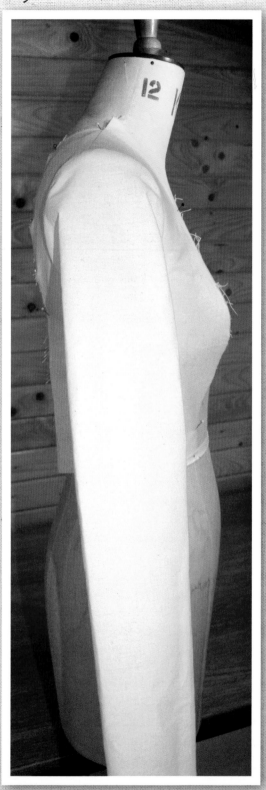

30 Turn the sleeve block to the right side and try on your model.

31 The sleeve should hang without any pulls as well as having a little fullness in the sleeve head.

32 Notice that – because we offset the bicep measurement – the sleeve hangs slightly forwards. Pin in and mark any adjustments that you feel are required.

You may want your sleeve looser or tighter. Re-cut, sew and try again if you feel it's necessary. Keep going until you have the perfect sleeve, then undo the sleeve, starch and press flat.

Now that your sleeve block is complete, you can use it to make all kinds of sleeve shapes. This will be explored later in the book.

By now, you have been introduced to all of the sewing and pattern-cutting techniques needed to make your three little black dresses.

If there was any principle or technique that you struggled with earlier, be sure to go back and do it again. Don't move on to making a little black dress until you feel completely and utterly confident.

When testing the teaching methods used in this book on friends, most of them couldn't wait to rush ahead and make something. Each of them reported that they moved on too quickly and had to revisit some of the sewing techniques again. I want you to be able to cut and make a dress with competence, without wasting expensive fabrics.

Students who don't believe they can follow sewing projects from books are normally the ones who move on to the next section too swiftly. Consequently, they loose confidence and put the book away. I want you to leave this book out the whole time, work slowly and thoroughly and enjoy the rewards when you unveil your very own, custom-made, fabulous little black dress.

The Dresses

'You can wear black at any time...You may wear it on almost any occasion; a "little black frock" is essential to a woman's wardrobe.'

CHRISTIAN DIOR

A Dress to Suit You

Now that you are equipped with a range of sewing techniques and have prepared your very own customized body block, it's time to move on to the exciting part: making your perfect little black dress.

Of course, some of you might be feeling so eager that you want to race ahead and make all of the dresses in this book. Others may want to make just the one for now, and see how they get on. If that's the case, make your first little black dress one that suits you perfectly. To identify the most flattering style, it is important to start by identifying your figure type.

I am constantly amazed that most women don't know their body shape. Read the descriptions in this section and be honest with yourself, Which category do you fit into? There is nothing wrong with any of the figure types, it's just a matter of proportion. If you know what type you are, you will also know the shapes that suit you. Play up your good bits!

Column
- Straight up and down, little size difference between bust, waist and hips.
- Tall and thin.
- Long rectangle shape.

Square
- Little variation between the bust, waist and hips.
- Shorter and fuller in figure than column body type.
- Square shape – no surprises there then!

Round
- Waist larger than hips and bust.
- Circle shape.

Top heavy
- Very full in the bust with smaller waist and hips.
- Triangle shape.

Bottom heavy
- Full in the hips and derriere and smaller in the bust and waist.
- Reverse triangle shape.

Hour glass
- About the same size hips and bust with a smaller waist.
- Figure eight shape.

Once you have identified your figure type, you need to know what shapes suit you. While there any aren't hard and fast rules – this exercise may encourage you to try something new.

If you are a Column

Aim to give the impression that your shoulders and hips are wider than they are, therefore cinching you in at the waist. Use a wide, scooped, round neckline and go for fuller skirt styles that finish just below the knee. Add a wide belt to cinch you in at the waist. Fit the bodice close to your body and wear a long sleeve that has some fullness or gathers at the shoulder then narrows towards the wrist. Keep shoe heels fairly low.

If you are a Square

Try to lengthen your shape by wearing longer lengths and straight, almost pencil-style, skirts. Try a wide 'v' neckline and plunge it as low as you dare. You can still get away with clothes that are quite fitted on the bodice. Sleeveless works best, but if you'd prefer not to reveal the tops of your arms, wear a short or three-quarter fitted sleeve. Try a wide belt to pull you in at the waist.

If you are Round

Deceive the eye into thinking that you have a waist. Wear long, fitted skirt styles with a loose bodice and, perhaps, a tie at the hips. Take inspiration from 20s- and 30s-style fashion. When wearing sleeves, make sure that they are very fitted and full length. Square or 'v' necklines and cross-over styles work best.

If you are Top Heavy

Wear sleeveless tops with 'v' necklines that narrow your shoulders and widen your hips. Wrap-over styles work well, but try not to add too many gathers to the bust area. Skirts should be full 'a' line or full-circle styles. Avoid wide belts as they pull you in and exaggerate your bust.

If you are Bottom Heavy

Wear round and scoop-shaped necklines to widen the top part of your body by wearing a gathered short or long sleeve. Wear fitted, long-length skirts to just above ankle length and wear high-heeled shoes whenever possible.

If you are an Hour Glass

You lucky girls, you can wear just about anything you want. Consider your height – wear shorter lengths if you are tall and longer lengths if short. Look at fashion magazines and find shapes and styles that attract you. See if you can work out the pattern shapes and construction methods.

The Little Black Dress

Be Creative: Make Your Own Designs

In the sewing techniques section of this book, there are lessons that we haven't used in the making of our little black dresses. These are included so that you can come up with your own designs beyond just the ones in this book. Try making the Marilyn dress but, instead of a zip, leave a wider opening in the back and lace it up. Drop the length down to the floor, add a split up the back seam and you have a wonderful column gown. Make the Greta dress, but instead of using ties, make a row of rouleau loops and fasten by adding some little buttons down one side. Try the Audrey dress with some gorgeous little cap sleeves.

Play around and come up with a style that's uniquely yours.

The three basic dress styles demonstrated in this book will suit all figure types; the main thing to consider is your proportions. The rule is simple: the fuller the figure, the longer a dress should be – this works to lengthen and thin the overall shape.

Then again, rules are made to be broken. You already know what suits you and the styles that you feel comfortable in. Show off your best features – if you have a killer cleavage, let the world see it!

Using the design and sewing methods in this book, the starting point will always be your toile. Look carefully at it during your fittings and ask yourself the following questions:

- Does it fit?
- Should it be longer or shorter?
- Should it be looser or tighter?
- Would it benefit from a lining? As well as hiding construction and raw seams, a good lining can smooth out any 'lumps and bumps' that you may have.
- What foundation garments am I going to wear with this dress?
- How am I going to accessorize it?

When you have answered all of these questions, you are pretty much there. Make up another toile, incorporating these changes, and look at it again.

Remember that every time you make a toile, you are practising your sewing skills.

Any construction problems that you may encounter will be sorted out on cheap calico. When you've found your perfect dress, it can be made again and again out of lots of different fabrics. It's well worth the time and effort it takes to get your dress just right.

Choosing Your Fabric

When selecting fabrics for your little black dress, there are many factors to consider. How often do you wear it? Will it be machine washed or dry cleaned? Is it easy to sew? To help you, I have compiled a list of suitable fabrics.

NATURAL FABRICS

Linen

I love linen. I love the crispness of its finish and the fact that it's easy to sew. But, most of all, I love the thing that most people hate about it: the creases. Creases are part of the beauty of linen, they make it special. Don't use it if you cannot stand the wrinkles or you will be pressing your dress every five minutes. Lining linen garments will slightly reduce the creasing.

Linen is a natural fibre, made from flax. On untreated fabric you can even smell the flax when you press it. It comes in different weights and tightness of weave – from the most delicate handkerchief linen to the stiff-as-a-board tea towels that your granny used to save for best. It's very stable so it sews well. Seams are easy to press, but can go shiny if you press too hard.

Linen is quite rigid, so cut on the straight grain it is ideal for tailored garments. Cut on the bias or cross grain, it takes on a wonderful drape quality that moulds itself to the body.

Being a natural fibre it takes to dye very well, so blacks are very black. With this said, colours can fade when overwashed; but that is yet another quality I like about it. It can be

Linen

washed either by hand or machine but be careful if it features a lining – this fabric often shrinks, pulling your dress out of shape. If in doubt, dry clean.

Wool Crêpe

Wool crêpe is probably my favourite tailoring fabric. It sews beautifully, presses crisply and works well when cut on either the straight grain or the bias.

Made from pure wool, it's very strong and durable and often outlives the wearer. It's produced by twisting the wool fibres tightly, giving the surface its characteristic rough and grainy texture. Wool crêpe hand washes quite well – use hair shampoo and conditioner – but I always recommend dry cleaning for best results.

You can also get 'wool mix' crêpe, made by mixing wool with other fibers such as polyester or acrylic. Wool mix can be quite good quality but, as there is little price difference from pure wool, why not treat yourself to the luxury of natural fibre?

There are also lots of other beautiful wool fabrics to look out for: cashmere, which comes from Kashmir goats; angora from the angora rabbit; and camel hair, from the underbelly of camels.

Silk

Silk is a natural product made from the cocoon of silkworms. The worms are either mulberry- or oak-fed. I can't really tell the difference between the two, but most believe that mulberry-fed is better.

Wool Crêpe

Silk Taffeta

The cocoons are boiled, unwound, spun, dyed and woven and that's all the treatment it requires. So, of all the fabrics, we can say that silk is the most natural.

Silk Jersey

Silk jersey is very expensive but worth every penny. Use for softer drape designs, where the heavy weight of the fabric will mould to fit every contour.

It is actually a knitted fabric and comes in 'single jersey' (stocking stitch with a 'knit' and a 'purl' side) or 'double jersey (a rib stitch, which looks the same on both sides). Single jersey tends to be difficult to sew as it rolls at the edges and frays very badly, while double jersey stays flat and doesn't fray quite as much. Because it's a knit, you need to finish the seams off very well – stitches can drop and cause a 'run' in the fabric. Be sure to use a 'stretch stitch' – a very fine zigzag – for best results. You will find this stitch setting on your machine. Coco Chanel and Jean Muir were regular users of silk double jersey.

Silk Crêpe

I love using silk crêpe, even though the fabric is quite thin, its weight gives it tremendous swing and drape qualities. One downside is that it can be difficult to

Silk Jersey

Silk Crêpe

cut and sew as it moves about when you are trying to work with it. To get around this problem, I often cut it out on the floor as the pile in the carpet helps to stabilize the slippery fabric. Cut on the bias it's even harder to control but it's well worth the extra effort for the luxurious result.

Silk Dupion

Silk dupion comes in either the Indian or Chinese varieties. Whereas Indian dupion is coarse and hand woven, the Chinese type is more likely to be machine made and, therefore, is much finer and tightly woven. Both qualities have 'slub' (a soft lump or unevenness) in the weave, giving an interesting surface texture.

As it is a natural fibre, dupion tends to crease, but don't let that put you off. In much the same way as linen, this is just part of the beauty. This unique fabric performs best when used with a lining, and is perfect for the strapless, boned little black dress.

Silk Charmeuse

You may see this advertised as satin-backed crêpe. It is shiny on one side, matt on the reverse and can be sewn using either side as the 'right side'; use both for some interesting texture contrasts. It also sews well on either the straight grain or bias.

Silk Dupion

MAN-MADE FABRICS

Acetate

Acetate is not very strong but can be extruded into lots of different thicknesses to take on the look of silks and other fabrics. It does not wear particularly well, and will melt with acetone and alcohol so be very careful with perfumes.

Acrylic

Acrylic is a soft, fine fibre with the bulk qualities and, some say, the handle of wool. I've used knitted acrylic fabrics to quite good effect but, as even the smallest amount of heat will 'kill' the handle of the fabric, it doesn't press particularly well.

Nylon

Nylon was used in the hosiery industry as an alternative to silk. It is strong and versatile but brings with it the dreaded 'static cling'. It works well when mixed with other fibres, especially in carpets, but is best avoided as a dressmaking fabric.

Polyester

I actually use polyester – there, I admitted it – but mostly as sewing thread, overlock 'bulking' or for lining fabrics. It works very well as a mix with cotton, which gives 'permanent press' properties and is excellent for shirts.

Rayon

Rayon is quite difficult to categorize as it is really a natural product. Coming from wood and being a cellulose fibre, it can be made to resemble most natural fibres, especially cotton or silk. You rarely see it in fabric shops and, when you do, it is mostly as a backing for velvet. It can shrink and warp when washed, so always pre-wash it before cutting to produce a washable, finished garment.

Lining fabrics

In general, dresses 'behave' better when lined. In couture sewing, we hardly ever produce an unlined garment. My mentor Mabel used to say that a good lining 'hides a multitude of sins'.

Use good quality lining of a weight that complements your top fabric. For a wool crêpe, use a medium-weight polyester satin lining. Try to find anti-static varieties to eliminate cling in the finished garment.

Interfacings and interlinings

Those of you who do a little sewing already will be surprised that I haven't mentioned interfacings or interlinings yet. The main reason is that, for most of the little black dresses in this book, we don't need them.

An interfacing is a piece of non-stretch fabric that stabilizes and strengthens a particular area of the garment, usually around the neck or down the front facings of a jacket. It can be sewn in but, most often in home sewing, the iron-on or fused variety is used.

Fused interfacings have a hot-melt glue bonded to them on one side so that the heat from an iron will stick the interfacing to the main fabric. I don't know of any couturiers who favour this type of interfacing. If we use it, as is often the case in tailoring, it is mostly the sew-in variety. For the purpose of this book, tailoring will be soft and fluid so there is no need to add any extra interfacing other than facings cut from the main fabric and lining.

Interlining is a fabric added to the main fabric to stabilize, strengthen and add weight to a finished garment. It is often cut and sewn with the top fabric as if it were one piece. In couture sewing, we will often baste two or even three layers of fabric together to get the weight that we want.

Making the right fabric choice will eliminate the need for an interlining in your little black dress.

I have only listed my favourite fabrics along with some you may wish to try. If you stick to natural fabrics you will get a much better finish. Whatever your fabric choice, go for the best that you can afford. If you use cheap fabric, you will get a cheap dress.

Useful Tip

An interfacing is a piece of non-stretch fabric that stabilizes and strengthens a particular area around a garment – usually around the neck or front facings.

How Much Fabric Will You Need?

How long is a piece of string? It's impossible to predict the exact amount of fabric you will need for your LBD – I don't know how wide you are or the kind of fabric you are using. One definite pearl of wisdom, though, is always buy more than you need!

The best way to work out the required fabric for any sewing project is to do a 'lay'. This involves literally laying out pattern pieces on a length of fabric the same width as the one you'll be using in your final project, and then measuring the length required. I always add at least 20% to this measurement to cover any mistakes or changes that may occur.

Fabrics come in all sorts of widths, so the first thing you need to establish is the width of your chosen material. Some are as narrow as 36 inches (91cm) and others are as wide as 90 inches (229cm).

Most of the dresses in this book are cut on the fold, so take a length of scrap material (I often use an old sheet) and cut it to half the width of your chosen fabric. Lay out your toile pieces on the edge of the fabric as if it were the fold. Make sure that your grain lines are all running in the same direction and are parallel to the edge.

Remember that, if you want to use bias strips to edge your dress, you need to allow enough fabric for this. Now measure the length of fabric needed, add about 20% for mistakes and round up to the nearest half-metre. Do the same for lining if required.

Embellishments

The shortest section of the book. In a word: don't! If you want to get lots of wear out of it, your little black dress should be simple. It's that simple. You want people to remember you, and how beautiful you looked, not that you were wearing the-same-old-dress-you-always-wear.

Accessorizing, on the other hand, is an altogether different thing to embellishing. Add some good pearls or one large piece of costume jewellery. Less is more.

So that's pretty much all you need to know in order to make your own little black dress. In the pages that follow, I have included three different styles.

The first dress is very simple, it is just an extended version of your body block; the second is a classic wrap dress with darts and a fuller skirt shape; and the third is a boned cocktail dress (this gets slightly more advanced). I have also included a little black jacket and hat to match the cocktail dress. I hope you like them and have a great time putting your creations together.

Between the three dresses and jacket, you will have all of the necessary techniques for designing your perfect dress. When you have finished the projects in this book, try to come up with your own designs and play with some of the new techniques you have learned. Go on, have a go, you may just surprise yourself.

Audrey

'Women can look like Audrey Hepburn by *flipping* out their hair, and *buying* the *large sunglasses*, and the *little sleeveless dresses*.'

Simple Shift Dress

Audrey

When you first look at this dress, it might appear to be quite advanced. So you may be surprised to learn that it is just the body block we have already sewn, with a few subtle alterations.

Think about what you have learned so far – for example, we have already inserted a concealed zip and used some bias binding. This will give you the confidence to make your first little black dress.

I am using a good quality Irish linen for this design, but you can use wool crêpe or even a heavy silk. We are not going to line this dress, so make sure that your fabric isn't see-through – unless you want to create a bit of a stir at the office!

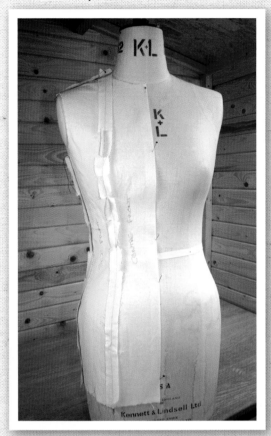

1

2a

2b

1 Start by making up half a body block in calico – see page 60.

2 Now mark in the neckline and armhole shape on the front and back (**2a & 2b**).

3 Mark in the waist and hip lines using elastic as we did earlier.

3

4a

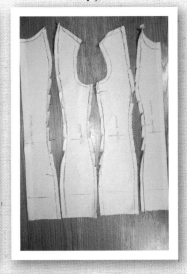

4b

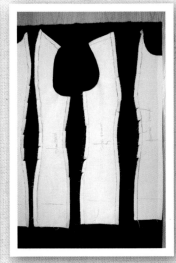

5

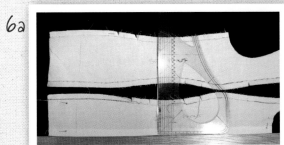

6a

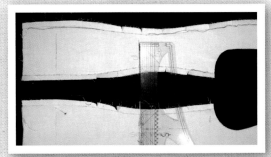

6b

4 Now undo the block, then press and starch it (**4a & 4b**).

5 Fold your main fabric in half, checking that the edges match exactly all the way down – this will ensure that the fold is on the straight grain of the fabric.

Place the pattern pieces onto the fabric exactly as you did for the body block – with the centre-front line along the fold.

6 To ensure that every pattern piece is on the straight grain of the fabric, check that your waist line mark is running at right angles to the fold line using your designer's square (**6a & 6b**).

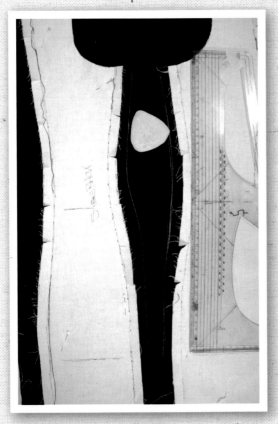

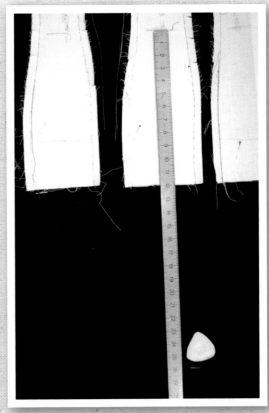

7 Using your tailor's chalk, mark an extra ⅜ inch (1cm) down both side seams to add ease. This will create 1½ inch (4cm) ease on the whole garment when constructed later.

8 Measure from the waist down to desired skirt length, and then mark this measurement – adding ⅜ inch (1cm) onto your fabric (**8a**). Next, draw a line at right angles to the fold line through this very same point (**8b**).

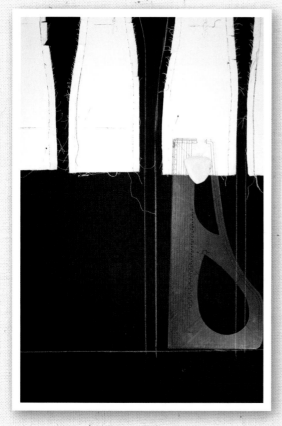

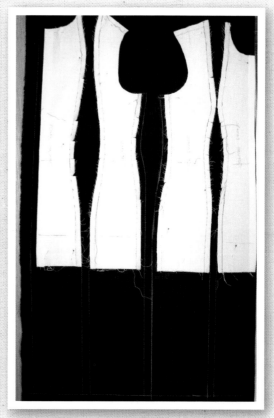

9 Extend the seams of the body block down to this line, making sure that the new lines are at right angles to the hem (**9a & 9b**).

There is no need to add seam allowance to the neck line or the armholes, as we will be bias-binding them later.

10 Neatly cut around the pattern pieces, keeping the body block pieces attached so that you can easily identify each one.

10

11a

11b

12a

12b

11 As we're not lining this dress, you will now have to add some finish to the inside seams. I used an overlocker but you can easily zigzag or overcast the fabric as we did on page 89 (**11a & 11b**).

12 Sew the side fronts to the centre front like we did with the body block (**12a & 12b**).

13 Now insert a 20 inch (50cm) zip into the centre-back seam (**13a & 13b**).

13a

13b

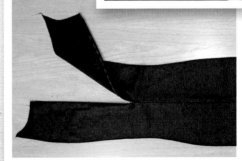

14

15a

15b

14 Add the side-back pieces and stitch the front to the back, down the side seams, then sew the shoulder seams.

15 The main body of your dress is now complete (**15a & 15b**).

17a

17b

Now you need to finish the armholes, neck edge and hem.

16 Bias-bind the neck and armholes. I used a satin bias for contrast, but you could make your bias out of the main fabric if you prefer (**16a & 16b**).

17 Now do a bias bagged hem (see section one, page 42) (**17a, 17b & 17c**).

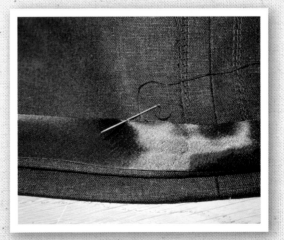

17c

And that's it, your first little black dress is ready to parade.

Greta

'It's not just *her* face, which is *gorgeous*. It's that she's *attractive* in a much *fuller* way than that.'

Classic Wraparound Dress

Greta

This style flatters every body type. Save your pattern because I'm sure once you make one, you'll want more. Try different lengths – a shorter version over jeans looks fabulous, as does ankle length worn with killer heels and chandelier earrings.

Your pattern will also be useful for garments other than just the little black dress project. Try just cutting out the bodice and sleeves. Make the ties wider and you have a funky waist length jacket. Or use a silk jersey and create an elegant 'ballet' top. You could also try a white silk crêpe for an elegant blouse. Just make up the skirt with the ties and it becomes a cool wrap skirt for the beach. Magic!

Are you starting to get the idea? Exciting, isn't it? The possibilities are endless. Your new wardrobe is only limited by your imagination.

Greta

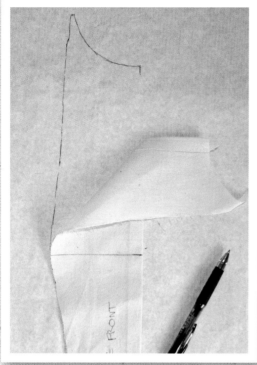

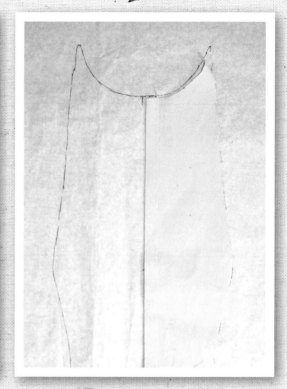

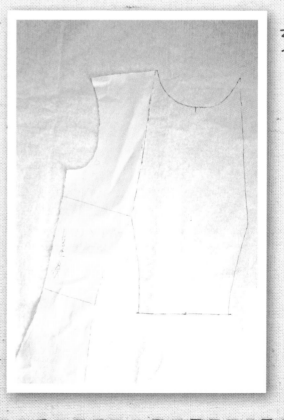

Let's make a start. First we need to create a paper pattern for this dress. Use the block pieces – from you the first body block made earlier.

1 Take a large sheet of pattern paper and lay the centre-front block piece centrally. Draw around the block to the waist line.

2 Flip the block piece over, line up the neck edge and the waist-line edge, then draw around again.

Now join up the waist-line points.

3 Take the side-front piece and place it along the centre-front pattern, joining up the shoulder dart.

4 Draw around the block piece to the waistline. Mark the waistline in.

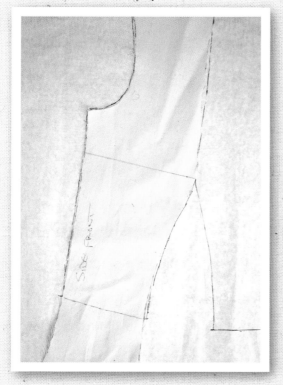

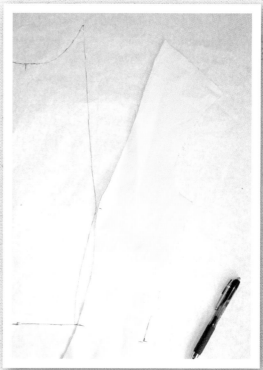

5 Flip the block over to the other side, then line up the bust points and waist-line point. Draw in the waist line and draw up the side seam for 1 inch (2.5cm).

6 Now draw a line from the lower curve of the neck line to the top of the line at the side seam (**6a & 6b**).

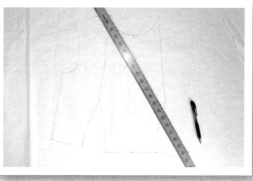

6a

6b

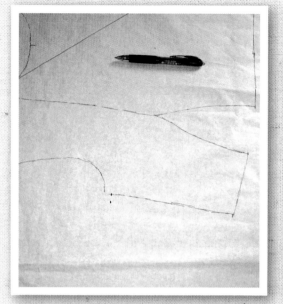

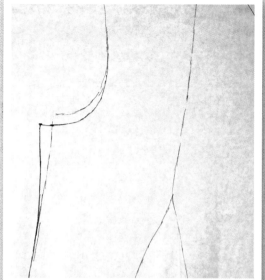

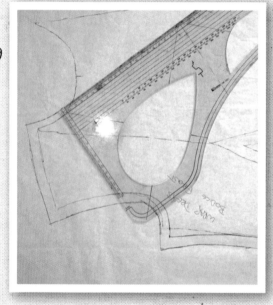

7 We don't want the sleeve to be too tight at the armhole, so mark about ⅜ inch (1cm) down from the underarm and then extend it out to the side for a further ⅜ inch (1cm).

8 Redraw the armhole edge and the side seam, curving in smoothly to existing lines.

9 Rub out all of the unwanted lines and add ⅝ inch (1.5cm) seam allowance all around, except the wrap edge. Add ⅜ inch (1cm) seam allowance to this edge as we are going to bias-bag it later.

10 Mark the pattern piece as 'wrap dress bodice front' and cut out.

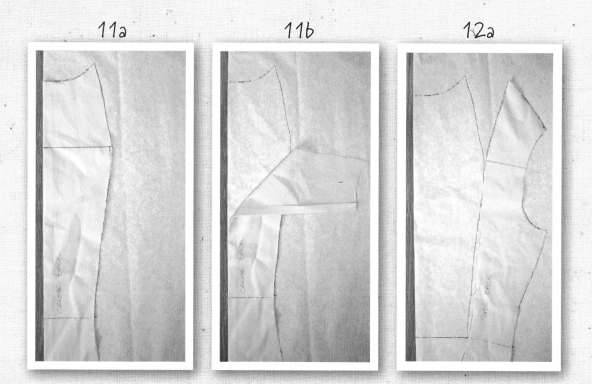

11 Now for the back. Place the centre-back block piece along the edge of the pattern paper and draw around it, then mark the waist line in (**11a & 11b**).

12 Place the side-back block piece alongside the centre-back piece, lining up the shoulder blade points and the waist line, and draw around (**12a & 12b**).

12b

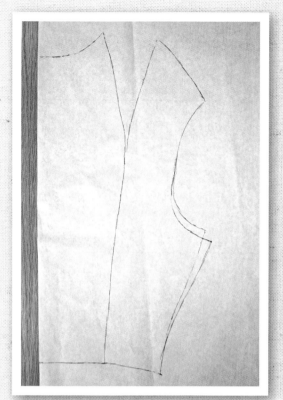

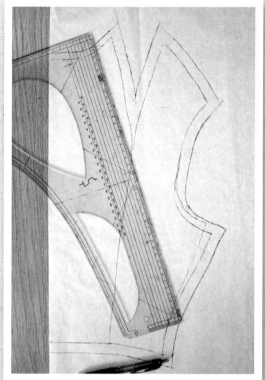

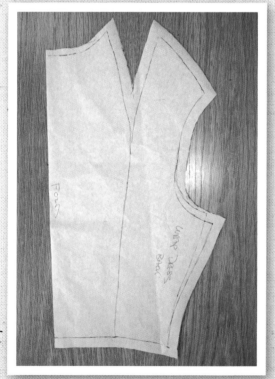

13 Extend the armhole line down and out –
just as we did for the front.

14 Rub out any unused lines and add seam
allowance to the waist, side and shoulder
seams including dart.

15 Mark the pattern piece 'wrap dress
back', mark the centre-back seam 'fold',
and cut out.

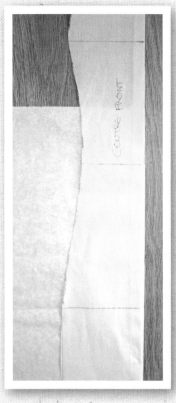

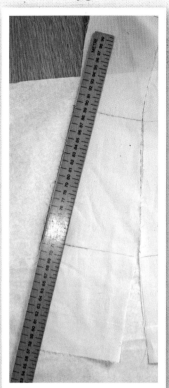

16 Now for the skirt pattern. Take a fresh piece of pattern paper and lay the centre-front block piece along one edge.

17 We are going to use the block from the waist line down. Now lay the side-block piece alongside it, matching up the waist lines and the hip lines to open up the hem.

18 Mark in the waist line and draw in the side seam, joining up the waist line to the fullest part of the hip.

19 Measure down the centre front from the waist line to the required skirt length.

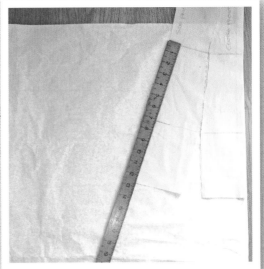

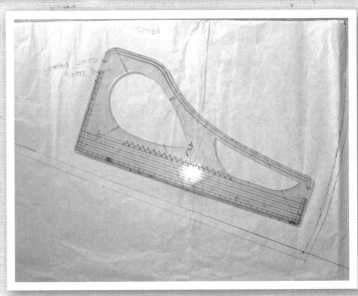

21a

21b

22

23

21 Repeat step 20 for the side seam and down an imaginary line, through where the block pieces join (**21a & 21b**).

22 Strike an arc to join the points – this is your hem line.

23 Add ⅝ inch (1.5cm) seam allowance to the waist line and side seam, and ⅜ inch (1cm) to the hem.

Mark the pattern piece 'wrap dress skirt front' and mark 'fold' on the centre-front line. As this is a wrap dress, we will need to cut two front pieces out of our fabric – when we get to that stage.

Now do exactly the same for the back skirt.

All that's left now is our sleeve pattern.

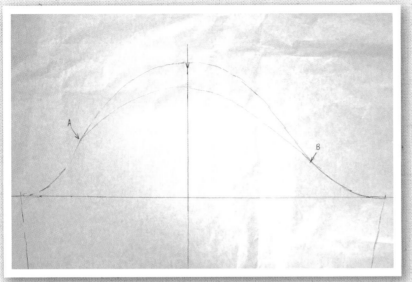

24

We are going to make the sleeve pattern using the same principles as section one. The only difference will arise when lifting the sleeve head. Because we want to leave some gather, lift it 1¼ inch (3cm) instead of ⅜ inch (1cm) .

24 Now draw the new sleeve head in, making nice smooth curves.

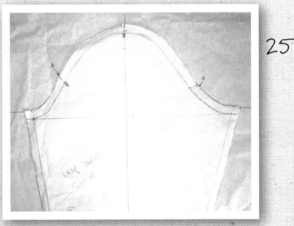

25

25 Add a seam allowance and mark the pattern piece 'wrap dress sleeve'. Remember to notch the shoulder and make a mark to indicate the back of the sleeve. Also, mark the points where the new fuller sleeve head shape meets the original sleeve head at the front and back (**A & B**). We are going to gather the sleeve head between these points.

26 And now that's a wrap for your wrap dress pattern!

26

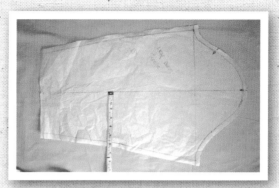

27

Before going any further, I strongly suggest making a toile for this dress so that any adjustments can be performed on cheap fabric. This will also give you valuable construction practice and sort out potential problems before cutting into the more expensive, main fabric.

Once the pattern is finished, this dress is actually quite easy to sew. There are no zips or buttons to worry about.

Fold your calico carefully in half, making sure the selvedges match up perfectly so your fabric lies on the 'straight grain'.

27 To ensure that the sleeve pattern is on the straight grain, measure in from the selvedge to the centre line of the sleeve in a couple of places and, when the measurements are all the same, your sleeve will be on the straight grain.

Lay your pattern pieces onto the calico with any pieces marked with 'fold' along the fold line of the fabric. Move the pieces around until you have as little waste as possible, but remembering to keep the pattern pieces on the straight grain. Remember that, as this is a wrap dress, you have to cut the front skirt piece twice.

28 In order to save fabric, a good trick is to flip the back piece over.

28

Useful Tip

It is only necessary to cut and sew the one sleeve for your toile.

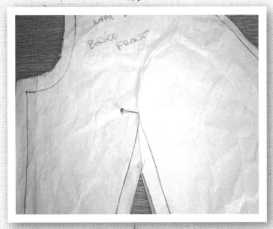

29a

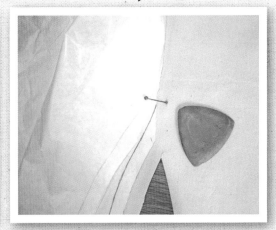

29b

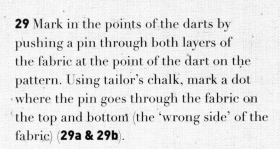

30a

30b

29 Mark in the points of the darts by pushing a pin through both layers of the fabric at the point of the dart on the pattern. Using tailor's chalk, mark a dot where the pin goes through the fabric on the top and bottom (the 'wrong side' of the fabric) (**29a & 29b**).

30 Sew in the darts on the two front and the back bodice pieces (**30a & 30b**).

31 Now press the front darts towards the side seam, and the back shoulder darts towards the centre.

31

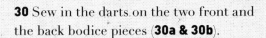

34a

32 Sew the front skirt pieces to the front bodice pieces at the waist seam.

33 Now sew the back skirt to the back bodice.

34 Sew down both side seams. On the real dress we will leave an opening – at the waistline on the right-hand side seam – for the tie. But there's no need to worry about this for our current toile. Now sew the shoulder seams (**34a & 34b**).

34b

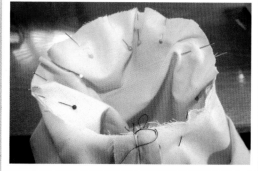

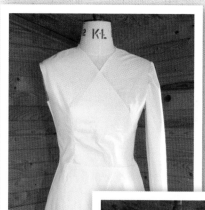

35 Sew up the sleeve seam and insert the sleeve as we did earlier (page 80), gathering the top of the sleeve head between the notches and being careful to ensure that the shoulder notch lines up with the shoulder seam (**35a, 35b & 35c**).

36 Try on your toile and then make any necessary adjustments (**36a & 36b**).

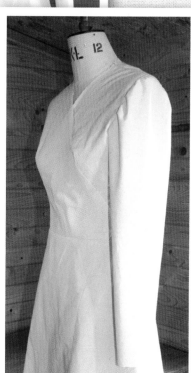

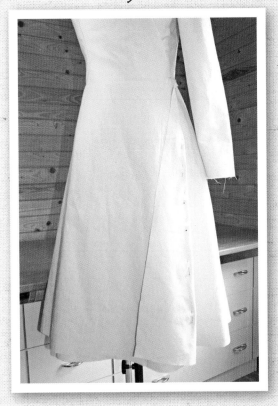

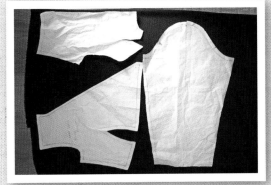

38a

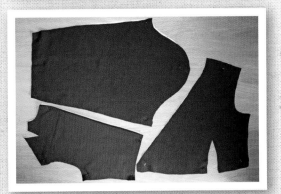

38b

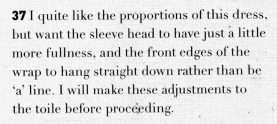

37 I quite like the proportions of this dress, but want the sleeve head to have just a little more fullness, and the front edges of the wrap to hang straight down rather than be 'a' line. I will make these adjustments to the toile before proceeding.

38 Once this is finished, we can undo the toile, starch and then transfer the alterations to the paper pattern before cutting out the main fabric (**38a & 38b**).

39 Finish off all of the seams except the neck, front edges and cuff edges.

39

41

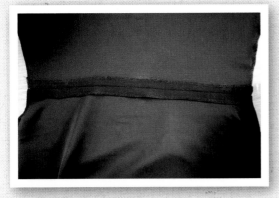

42a

40 Make up the main fabric just as you did earlier with the toile (**40a**), only this time be sure to leave a ¾ inch (2cm) opening in the side seam at the waist line – on the right-hand side – for the tie (**40b**).

42b

41 Overlock or overcast the hem edge. Turn the hem to the inside by folding it in – just over the width of the overlocking – and then stitch close to the edge.

42 Sew up the sleeve seams, insert and sew to the bodice (**42a & 42b**). See page 80 for guidance if you've forgotten how.

43a

43b

44a

44b

43 To make your ties, cut two strips of fabric 3 inch (8cm) wide and the full length of your fabric. Fold in half width ways and stitch a ⅜ inch (1cm) seam across the short edge, then down the long edge (**43a & 43b**).

44 Clip the corner at an angle (**44a**), turn the tie through to the right side and press. Repeat for the other tie (**44b & 44c**).

44c

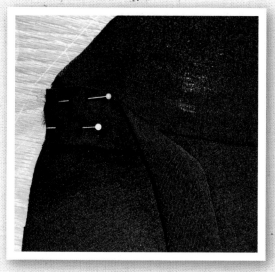

45

46a

46b

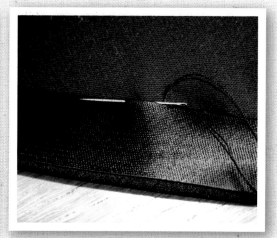

47

45 With right sides together, pin the open edge of the ties to the front-waist edges of the bodice.

46 Now bias-bag up the front edge – stitch over the tie, around the neck edge and down the other side (**46a & 46b**).

47 Fold in and press, turning in the bottom edge of the bias to make a neat finish, and hand stitch into place.

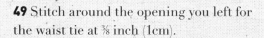

48 Turn in and sew the cuffs just as you did earlier for the hem.

49 Stitch around the opening you left for the waist tie at ⅜ inch (1cm).

Now wear and enjoy!

Marilyn

'What do

I wear *in bed*?

Why,

Chanel No. 5,

of course.'

Strapless Boned Dress

Marilyn

Miss Monroe opitimized Hollywood glamour and old-world grace, and so does this stunning LBD. Follow Marilyn's example by showing off a frightfully sexy flash of décolletage – you might even snare a millionaire.

We will now make our first attempt at lining a dress. Earlier, I quoted my old mentor Mabel: 'a good lining hides a multitude of sins'. Actually, a good lining can save a garment from ruin – you don't have to finish your seams off because they will be 'bagged' inside the lining.

To make things a little more interesting, we are also going to add some boning to give our dress extra support. Don't panic, just follow the instructions systematically and you will be just fine.

First of all, as with the previous exercise, let's make the pattern.

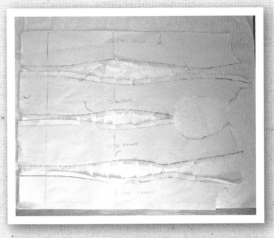

1

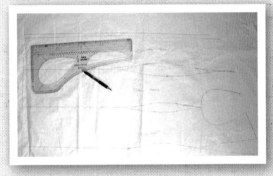

3a

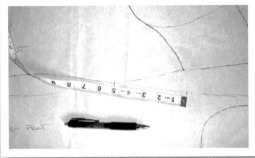

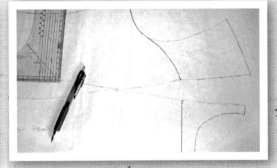

3c

1 On a large piece of pattern paper, lay your block pieces side by side (just as we did for the linen dress), making sure the centre front is on the edge of the pattern paper. Next, place down the side front, side back and centre back.

2 Draw around all of your block pieces and extend them down to the required skirt length plus ¾ inch (2cm), adding a seam allowance to the centre-back seam. As this is a tight-fitting dress, there is no need to add ease allowance to the side seams.

3 Draw in the front-top shape – start from the underarm point – then curve over the bust. Make sure that the length from the bust point to the top shape is the same for the centre and side-fronts (**3a, 3b & 3c**).

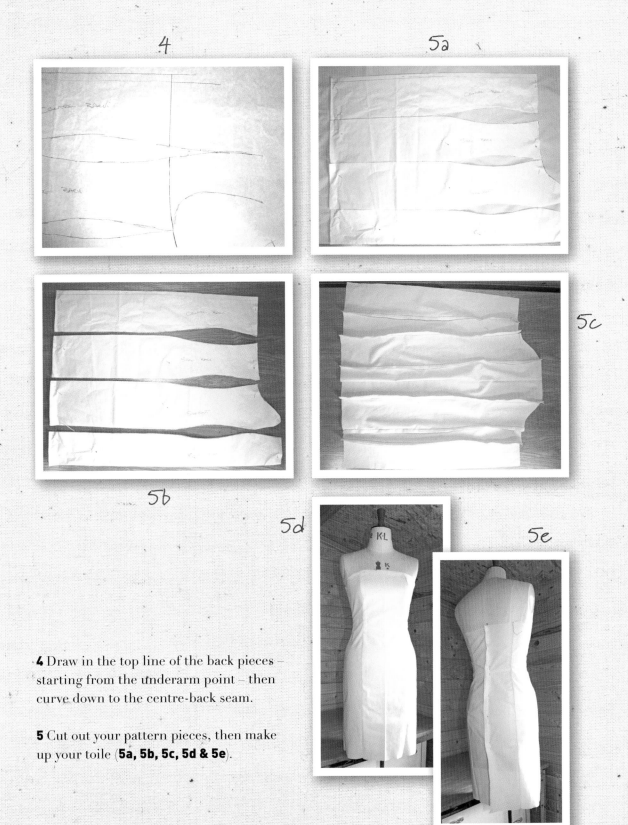

4 Draw in the top line of the back pieces – starting from the underarm point – then curve down to the centre-back seam.

5 Cut out your pattern pieces, then make up your toile (**5a, 5b, 5c, 5d & 5e**).

6a

6b

7

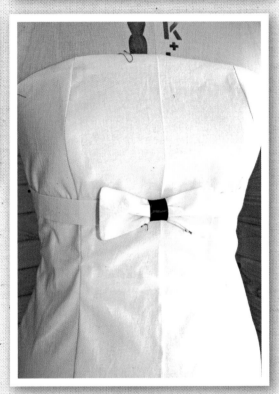

8

6 Cut a length of calico on the bias 3 inches (8cm) wide, long enough to fit the front-under-bust length. If you cut this a little longer, you can adjust it to fit later.

Cut two rectangles to the length and the width you want your bow, plus seam allowance. Now stitch around the rectangles, leaving a small gap so that you can turn it through. Turn the bow right sides out and press – as this is only a toile there is no need to sew up your opening as you will do with your LBD (**6a & 6b**).

7 Gather the centre of the bow and wrap a small piece of bias around to secure to the centre of the tie.

8 Attach to the toile, check that you like the proportions, and mark the placement.

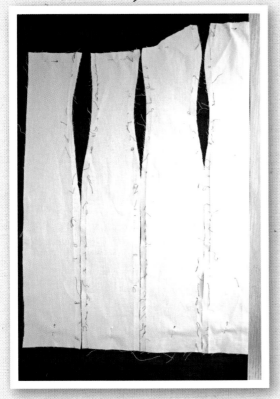

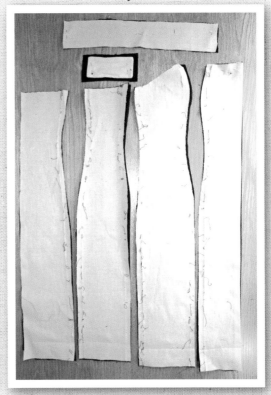

9 When you are happy with the fit and proportion of your toile, unpick it, press and then cut out your pattern pieces from the main fabric. For this exercise, I have used a crisp silk dupion, but a wool crêpe or linen would also work nicely. Now cut out the same pieces in your lining, with the length ⅜ inch (1cm) shorter (**9a, 9b & 9c**).

Make up the lining first, in exactly the same way as the toile. Now we are going to add some bones. I have used white boning so that you can see it, but black rigiline boning would be better for your LBD.

9c

10a

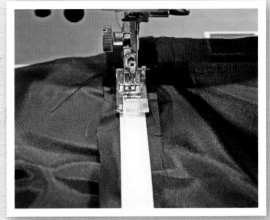

10b

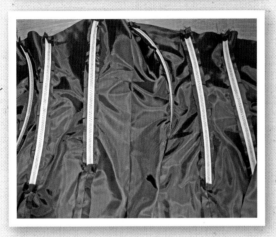

10c

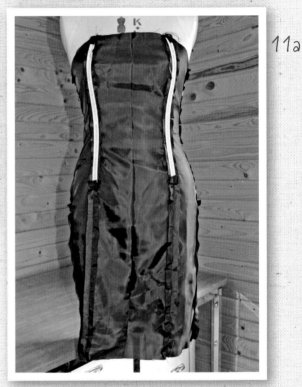

11a

10 Measure along from the very top of the centre-front pattern down to about 4 inches (10cm) past the waist line. Cut six pieces of boning to this measurement.

Remember to cover the ends of your boning – as we did in section one (page 47). Sew from the top seam and zigzag all six bones in place (**10a, 10b & 10c**).

11 Sew the centre-back seam of the lining, leaving the length of the zip open (**11a**). I have also added a label to my dress (**11b**).

11b

12a

12b

12c

12d

12 Make up the band and bow as we did for the toile (**12a, 12b, 12c & 12d**).

13 Sew the front of the main dress together before pinning the bow band into place (**13a & 13b**), making sure it's straight.

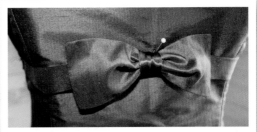

13a

13b

The Dresses 149

14

15a

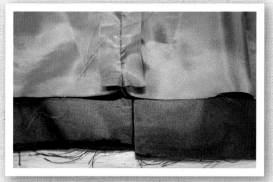

15b

14 Add a concealed zip into the back seam.

Now join the front and back pieces of the dress together.

15 Place the main dress inside the lining with the 'right sides' together. Match up the hem seams and sew a ⅜ inch (1cm) allowance around the hem line (**15a & 15b**).

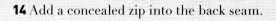

Useful Tip

The right side (front) of a concealed zip actually looks more like the wrong side (back) of the zip.

 16

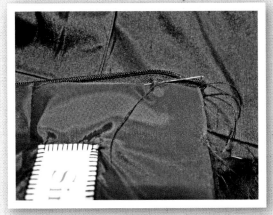

17a

17b

16 Turn through to the 'right side' and pin the seams together around the top of the dress.

17 Turn in the centre-back lining seams ⅝ inch (1.5cm) and stitch into place along the zip tape (**17a & 17b**).

18a

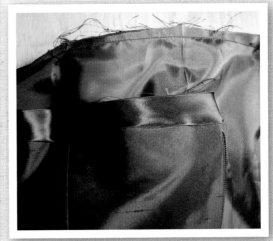

18b

18c

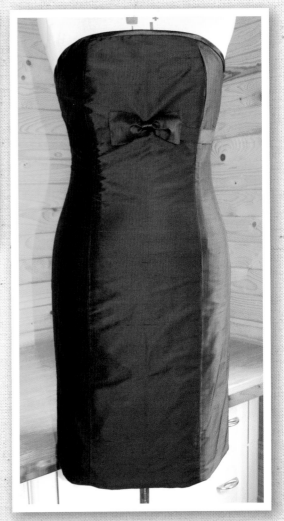

18 Now we need to bind the top of the dress. I'm using satin bias but you can cut your binding out of the main fabric if you wish (**18a, 18b & 18c**). Refer to page 44 if you've forgotten how.

All you need to do now is press your dress and it's ready to parade.

The Little Black Jacket

'A girl should be two things:
classy and fabulous.'

COCO CHANEL

The Little Black Jacket

You will be amazed by how easy this little jacket is to sew. Save the pattern as you will certainly want to make it again. If you take time to make your pattern and toile, the actual jacket is a breeze.

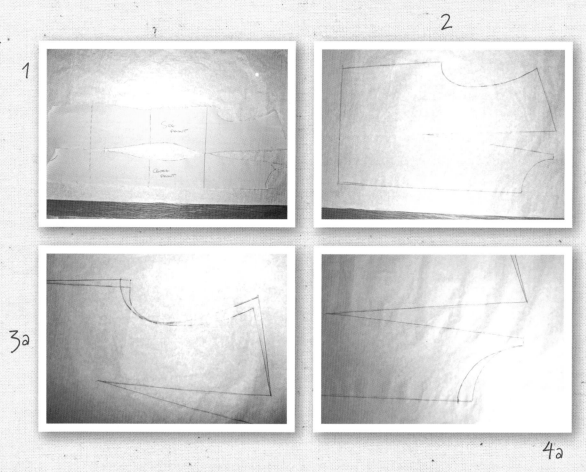

1 Start by placing your centre-front and side-front blocks onto your pattern paper, with the bust and hip points together.

2 Draw around your block pieces to just past the waist, then mark the waist line in. There's no need to add waist darts.

3 As we need an additional ⅜ inch (1.5cm) (ease for the side seams, draw in the existing seam – which already includes allowance. Drop the waist line down by about 1½ inch (4cm) to make a new hem line. Lower the underarm point by about ⅝ inch (1.5cm) and extend the shoulder point out by the same amount. Now draw in your new armhole shape.

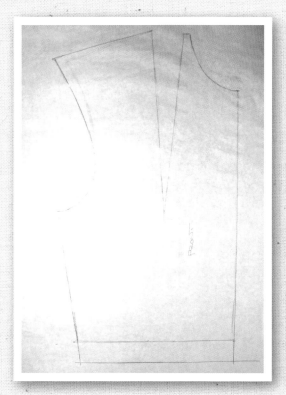

4b

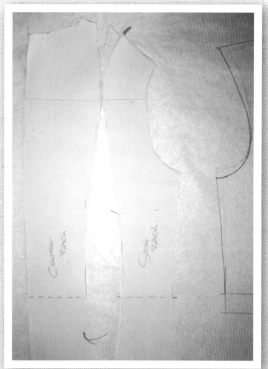

5

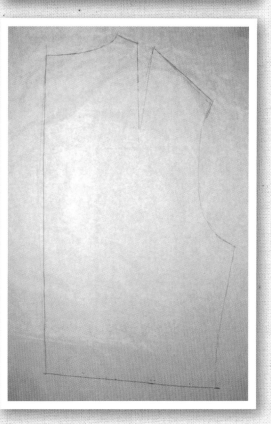

6

4 Shift the centre-front neckline point down ¾ inch (2cm) and draw in the new shape (**4a & 4b**).

5 Place the side-back block piece alongside, lining up the waist lines, hip points and side seams, and then draw in.

6 Place the centre back with shoulder and hip points touching, and draw in.

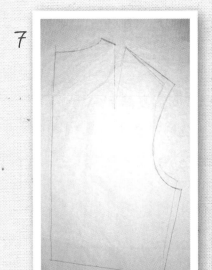

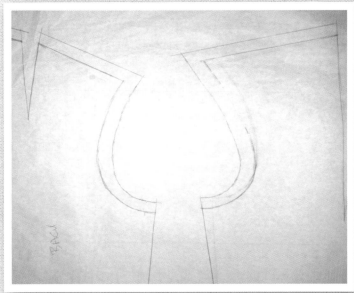

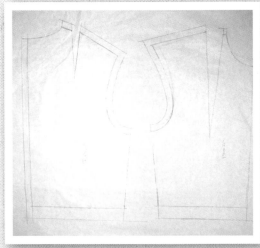

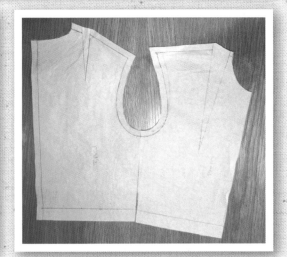

7 Lower the armhole point and extend the shoulder seam, just as we did for the front.

8 Add seam allowance to the centre back, armhole and shoulder seams and then cut these pieces out (**8a, 8b & 8c**).

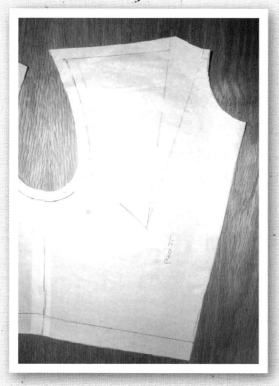

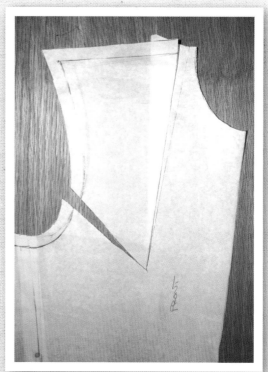

10a

10b

Okay now, for something new, we are going to manipulate some darts.

9 Draw a line from the armhole edge to the bust point and cut along it. Cut down one of the bust dart lines and open up slightly.

10 Close the bust dart by bringing the lines together and taping – you will notice that a new dart has opened up at the armhole edge (**10a & 10b**).

Congratulations, you have just manipulated your first dart.

Earlier in the book, when we made our first body block, I mentioned that it didn't really matter where the shoulder-to-bust dart was placed. Now you can see why: it can easily be moved around.

11

12

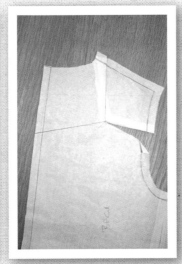

13a

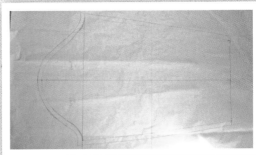

13b

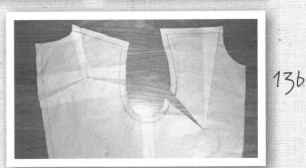

13c

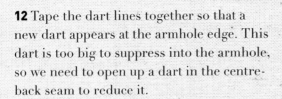

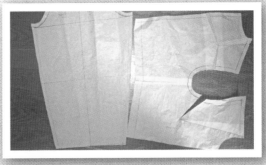

13d

11 Now we are going to swing the back shoulder dart into the back seam. Draw a line from the armhole edge to the bottom of the shoulder dart point and cut along this line. Next, you need to cut one of the shoulder dart lines.

12 Tape the dart lines together so that a new dart appears at the armhole edge. This dart is too big to suppress into the armhole, so we need to open up a dart in the centre-back seam to reduce it.

13 Draw a line from the centre-back seam to the same point as before. Cut along this line and open up the dart in the back seam to reduce the dart in the armhole (**13a**).

As you can see, these new darts are small enough to blend into the armhole and centre-back seams. Tape some paper under the darts and re-cut the seam lines (**13b**). Now that your bodice pattern is finished, we can make a sleeve pattern (**13c**), as we did on page 80, and cut out (**13d**).

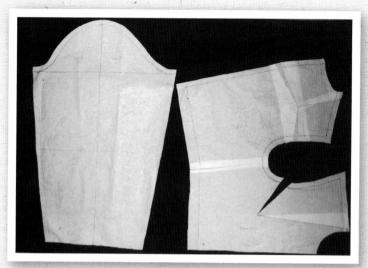

14 Cut out pattern pieces from the main fabric and do the same for the lining.

15 Mark in the dart points, then clip the edges of the darts into the seam allowance – to mark the darts – as well as your underarm side seam-point.

16 Make up your main fabric and lining by sewing in the darts and stitching the shoulder seams.

16

17a

17b

18

17 Assemble your sleeves and sew them in – just as we did with the sleeve toile on page 161 (**17a & 17b**).

18 Cut the hem of the lining ¾ inch (2cm) shorter so that it doesn't drop below the main fabric when wearing your jacket.

19 With 'right sides' together, sew a ⅜ inch (1cm) seam across the hem from the front edge to the front edge (**19a & 19b**).

Turn the lining to the inside and push the lining sleeves down the main sleeves. Because we have cut the lining shorter, you will see that the main fabric turns to the inside at the hem.

19a

19b

20

Now we want to stop the lining from slipping down when you wear your jacket. Reach inside the centre front, in between the main and lining fabrics, and grab the seams under the arm. Next, place the seams together, then sew two or three stitches forwards and backwards inside the allowance to hold the lining in place.

Do the same at the shoulder-to-sleeve seams.

20 All that is left to complete your jacket is to bias-bind the neck, front edges and cuffs just as we did on page 116.

And voilà, the perfect little black jacket to go with the perfect little black dress.

The Little
Black Hat

'Cock your hat –
angles are attitudes.'

FRANK SINATRA

The Little Black Hat

No glamorous outfit is complete without a little hat or fascinator. In the spirit of this book, let's make our own. Whether you are going to the races or just dressing to the nines for no occassion at all, this hat is simple to make yet sophisticated to wear.

1a

1b

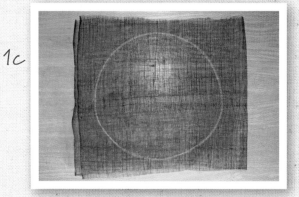

1c

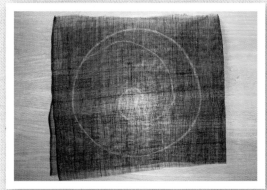

2

You will need:

- About 39 inches (1 metre) of sinamay – millinery fabric from specialist suppliers
- Clear flexible headband or plastic hair comb
- Hot glue gun
- Handful of jet beads
- Satin bias binding.

1 Lay out a double layer of sinamay and use a large dinner plate to mark out a circle – trace around it with tailor's chalk (**1a, 1b & 1c**).

2 Now draw in a spiral within the circle, like a snail shell design.

The Little Black Dress

3a

3b

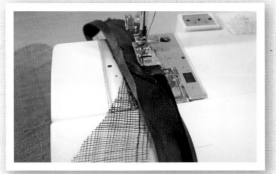

4a

4b

4c

4d

4e

3 Cut around the circumference and along the spiral for both layers (**3a & 3b**).

4 Bias-bind the outer edge of one of the spirals and hand sew into place (**4a, 4b, 4c, 4d & 4e**).

5a

5b

6a

6b

5 Place the bound and unbound spirals together on top of each other, and start to twist them inwards, stitching through the layers at the base as you go (**5a & 5b**).

At this point, the hat will take on a life of its own. Don't panic, just relax and let the fabric do the work for you. It is amazing what happens as you start to twist. It will soon become obvious why I call the final result the 'cup and saucer'.

6 Using a hot-melt glue gun, stick the base of the fascinator to the band or hair comb. Now glue a few jet beads to the centre of your design – anywhere along the spiral – be creative and add as few or as many as you please, but remember that 'less is more' (**6a & 6b**).

And there you have it, the perfect little black hat for your perfect little black dress.

I hope that you have enjoyed the journey
of making your own little black dress; if only
I could be there to help you along the way.
You never know, if you wish really hard,
the sewing fairy might just drop by. . .

Glossary

Bagged in When all the rough side seams and hems are hidden inside a lining, making the garment as neat as the outside.

Bias The diagonal grain of a fabric; neither on the straight length or width grain of a fabric, but running on the 'cross grain'.

Blade point The highest point of the shoulder blade.

Bodice The top part of a dress that fits the torso.

Body block A perfect fabric rendition of the body , usually made out of calico. We use this for drafting patterns for the actual garment.

Boning A rigid or semi-rigid piece of polyester, acrylic or metal that is either sewn directly onto a seam, or placed inside a casing. Used to create stiffness or support on any part of a garment. Most often used in strapless dresses or in corsetry.

Bust point The highest part of the bust, usually in the centre at the nipple.

Calico A stiff, un-dyed cotton used for making body blocks and toiles. Known as quilter's cotton or unbleached muslin in the U.S.

Couture Literally, 'seam'. In modern times, the term is used to describe the top end of fashion and dress-making where most of the work is done by hand.

Cross grain *See* **Bias**.

Dart A method of suppressing fabric when a full seam is not required.

Designer's square A set square with cut-out curves; used in pattern cutting and drafting.

Draft When we draw a pattern onto pattern paper or directly onto fabric, we are drafting a pattern.

Dress stand Often referred to as a tailor's dummy, it is a model of a body that we can use to fit garments.

Ease The amount of extra fabric incorporated into a garment to make the desired fit.

Facing A piece of fabric that sits on the inside of the garment, usually down the front edges or around the neck or armholes.

Fascinator A large hair accessory or small hat.

Fitting When fitting a garment, we are checking the fit and hang before making any necessary adjustments.

French seam A seaming method that 'bags in' raw edges.

Hem The finish on the bottom edge of a garment.

Interfacing A non-woven fabric used to stiffen or add support to various areas of a garment.

Invisible zip A special type of zip that is concealed inside a seam, rendering it 'invisible'.

Iron shield A plastic or acrylic cover that fits onto the bottom of an iron; used to protect delicate fabrics.

LBD The little black dress.

Lining The fabric used for the inside of a garment.

Modelling The process of draping calico onto a stand or directly onto the body in order to make a pattern.

Neck line The shape or part of the garment that fits around the neck.

Notch A method of marking the fabric within the seam allowance by snipping into it with the points of scissors.

Off-set The amount that we move a point from the centre line.

Overcast A method of seam finish; closely replicating an overlocked edge but without cutting a fabric as the edge is sewn.

Overlock A method of seam finish that neatens the edge of a fabric whilst cutting off the raw edges.

Pattern Used as a marker to cut out your fabric; usually made of paper or calico.

Right side The side of a fabric that will show on the outside of a finished garment.

Rigiline A trade name for polyester/nylon boning; used to stiffen or support areas of your garment.

Rouleau A thin tube of fabric used for loops or straps in fine dresses and lingerie.

Run off Letting your machine sew off the edge of a fabric – usually in darts.

Seam Where two or more pieces of fabric are joined.

Seam allowance The amount of fabric used for a seam. Usually 1 or 1.5cm in from the edge of a fabric.

Selvedge The thicker, stronger edge of the fabric.

Serge *See* **Overlock**.

Sinamay A specialist millinery fabric.

Sleeve block The pattern for making the sleeve of a garment.

Sleeve head The curved top edge of a sleeve that fits into the shoulder edge of the bodice,

Snip A little cut made with the points of your scissors.

Straight grain The grain of fabric running in the same direction as either the weft or warp threads: top-to-bottom or side-to-side.

Supression The amount of fabric removed from an area of a garment in order to facilitate fit.

Tailoring shears Large scissors used for just cutting fabric.

Toile A rough calico rendition of a finished garment.

Wrong side The side of a fabric that will not be seen on a finished garment – in other words, it is worn on the inside.

Zigzag A stitch shape that swings from side to side.

Acknoweledgements

GMC Publications would like to thank

Chris Gloag, and his assistant Guillaume Serve, for the fashion photography.

Sephora Venites from Zone Models.

AJ for make-up.

Simon Henry for hair.

The following companies for allowing us to photograph in their shops, and for all their help:

CHOCCYWOCCYDOODAH
24 Duke Street,
Brighton, BN1 1AG

COLIN PAGE ANTIQUARIAN BOOKS
36 Duke Street,
Brighton,
East Sussex,
BN1 1AG

COLOGNE & COTTON
13 Pavilion Buildings,
Castle Square,
Brighton,
East Sussex,
BN1 1EE

GUNN'S FLORISTS
6 Castle Square,
Brighton,
East Sussex,
BN1 1EG

The following, for lending us props and accessories:

DAVID CLULOW
25 East Street,
Brighton,
East Sussex,
BN1 1HL
For the glasses on pages 1, 2, 19, 21, 59, 108-9, 117, 119, 120-1 and 139.

FARROW & BALL *for wallpaper backgrounds.*

LK BENNETT *for the shoes on pages 119 and 153.*

PHILIP PARFITT at Wardrobe (see address below) *for the vintage jewellery on pages 1, 19, 59, 93, 107, 119, 139, 141, 142-3, 153, 155 and 163.*

WARDROBE
51 Upper North Street,
Brighton,
East Sussex,
BN1 3FH
For the accessories on pages 1, 107 and 139.

Author's Acknowledgements

A big thanks to Jonathan and Gerrie for believing in me; to my lovely antipodean editor Louise (tall hugs, fat hugs), to Rachel (who is just too fabulous), Gilda, Hedda and everyone at GMC for making me feel very welcome and helping with the 'birthing' process of my first book.

Thanks to 'Mr Norm' for helping me buy the right photographic equipment.

I must also mention Mabel Zsharga, who ignited my passion for creating couture outfits. Thanks to Sarah for looking after my shop, giving me extra time for this project. Special thanks to Martina Enwright, my house model and muse, and to Sue Webster and those who tested out the exercises in this book – you

know who you are. Thanks to New Home and Toyota Machines, cheapfabrics.com, Kliens haberdashery, Macculloch and Wallice of London.

And last, but certainly not least, to Clive – my civil partner and best friend. He gave me support and encouragement, looked after things at home while I spent hours in my studio, and patiently read through countless rewrites. You are the one who keeps my feet firmly on the ground, thank you.

And to you, my readers. Thanks for buying this book. I hope you enjoyed learning from it. Wear your little black dress with pride.

Love, as always, Simon x

Suppliers

Fabrics

WWW.MACCULLOCH-WALLIS.CO.UK
For beautiful, top-end fabrics as well as millinery supplies and tools. Expect to pay top-end prices, but it's well worth it.

WWW.CHEAPFABRICS.CO.UK
Good quality fabrics at very reasonable prices. This is an excellent site for silks and calico.

WWW.WHALEYS-BRADFORD.LTD.UK/RANGE_FABRICS.HTM
Top quality wool crêpe. Available in black and navy or undyed.

WWW.ABAKHAN-ONLINESHOP.CO.UK/ACATALOG/DRESS.HTML
Always lots of clearance lines; keep visiting the site for the best deals.

WWW.CANDH.CO.UK/
A good, all-round selection of fabrics at very keen prices.

Pattern-making supplies

WWW.MORPLAN.CO.UK
An excellent store for design equipment and consumables.

WWW.SHOBENFASHIONMEDIA.COM/
For patterns, books and designer set squares.

Machines

WWW.HOME-SEWING.COM/ENG/INDEX.PHP
For Toyota sewing and overlock machines.

WWW.BROTHERMACHINES.COM

WWW.JANOME.CO.UK

WWW.HUSQVARNAVIKING.COM

WWW.PFAFF.COM

WWW.BERNINA.COM

Index

A

To request a full catalogue of GMC titles, please contact:

**GMC Publications Ltd, Castle Place, 166 High Street,
Lewes, East Sussex, BN7 1XU, United Kingdom
Tel: 01273 488005 Fax: 01273 402866 www.gmcbooks.com**